Elite • 153

The Australian Army in World War II

Mark Johnston · Illustrated by Carlos Chagas

Consultant editor Martin Windrow

First published in Great Britain in 2007 by Osprey Publishing,
Midland House, West Way, Botley, Oxford OX2 0PH, UK
443 Park Avenue South, New York, NY 10016, USA
E-mail: **info@ospreypublishing.com**

ISBN 978 1 84603 123 6

Editor: Martin Windrow
Page layouts by Ken Vail Graphic Design, Cambridge, UK
Typeset in Helvetica Neue and ITC New Baskerville
Index by Glyn Sutcliffe
Originated by PPS Grasmere, Leeds, UK
Printed in China through World Print Ltd.

07 08 09 10 11   10 9 8 7 6 5 4 3 2 1

A CIP catalogue record for this book is available from the British Library

FOR A CATALOGUE OF ALL BOOKS PUBLISHED BY OSPREY MILITARY
AND AVIATION PLEASE CONTACT:

North America:
**Osprey Direct, c/o Random House Distribution Center, 400 Hahn Road,
Westminster, MD 21157**
Email: **info@ospreydirect.com**

All other regions:
Osprey Direct UK
PO Box 140, Wellingborough, Northants NN8 2FA, UK
Email: **info@ospreydirect.co.uk**

Buy online at **www.ospreypublishing.com**

Acknowledgements

My sincere thanks to the staff of the Australian War
Memorial, especially Garth Pratten, Brad Manera, Peter
Stanley, Jane Peek, Peter Burness, Joanne Smedley, Hank
Nelson and Bob Courtney. I am also grateful to Paul
Handel, Peter Bannigan, Phillip Bradley, David Pearson,
Robyn Smithwick, and to veterans Alwyn Shilton, Noel Hall,
Alan Hooper, Jim McAllester, Bill McEvoy and Alan
Macfarlane. Special thanks to Martin Windrow.

Artist's note

Readers may care to note that the original paintings from
which the colour plates in this book were prepared are
available for private sale. All reproduction copyright
whatsoever is retained by the Publishers. All enquiries
should be addressed to:

Carlos Chagas *mailto:crchagas@terra.com.br*

The Publishers regret that they can enter into no
correspondence upon this matter.

TITLE PAGE **Australian troops leave their American-manned
'amtracks' for a patrol in North Borneo in June 1945. The
man advancing at centre wears his water bottle on his chest
between his pouches. The heavily laden soldier in the
centre foreground, with a white mug on his haversack, is
19-year-old Pte Varischetti, who would be killed in action
within days of this photo being taken. (Australian War
Memorial 018680)**

THE AUSTRALIAN ARMY IN WORLD WAR II

INTRODUCTION

Corporal McDonnell of 2/5th Infantry Battalion, 17th Infantry Brigade, 6th Australian Division smiles for the camera after a fighting patrol during the 1943 Wau-Salamaua campaign in New Guinea. He wears green camouflage face paint and – like many others at this late stage of the campaign – unorthodox headgear, apparently crowned with a piece of camouflage net. McDonnell was wounded in both Syria and New Guinea, and Mentioned in Despatches. (Australian War Memorial 015693)

The character of the Australian Army of World War II owed much to its Great War counterpart. In World War I the all-volunteer Australian Imperial Force had first won fame in the ill-fated Gallipoli campaign of 1915. On the Western Front in 1916–18 the AIF came to be employed as an elite force; it contributed substantially to Allied victory and garnered numerous honours and decorations, but at the cost of appalling losses. Memories of the 60,000 Australian dead haunted the country in the inter-war period, helping to foster a deep antipathy to war and a decline in armed forces funding. When a Second World War did come, Australia dutifully joined Britain on 3 September 1939, but there was no repetition of the enthusiastic mass enlistments of 1914. Those who did consider signing up for the Second AIF were conscious of the standard set by the First AIF; this encouraged some, but daunted others.

Nevertheless, from the time of the first victories in Libya in 1941, the Second AIF maintained the traditions of 1914–18 and established new traditions of its own. There were reverses, in Greece, and on various islands of doom such as Crete and Singapore. However, in the siege of Tobruk, the battle of El Alamein, the fighting along the Kokoda Track and on innumerable other battle-fields, the Australians established a high reputation among both their allies and their enemies. Like the First AIF, the Second was under Australian command, and was required to stay together as far as this was practical within the campaigns that the British directed in 1940–42. From the time of Japan's entry into the war at the end of 1941, Australian troops were fighting closer to home than ever before, as the long-held Australian fear of a 'yellow peril' became more terrifying and substantial. In the campaigns that followed the United States replaced Britain as the great ally into whose broader plans Australia fitted its own. None the less, in its war against Japan

At Bardia in Libya in January 1941, soldiers like these men of the Second Australian Imperial Force established a new tradition for the Australian Army. Their woollen service dress, helmets, rifles and sword bayonets are all reminiscent of their Great War predecessors of the First AIF. The soldier at right wears a British sleeveless leather jerkin, one of 11,500 issued on the eve of battle; some Italian troops at Bardia thought that these must be bulletproof... (Australian War Memorial P00643.007)

in 1942–45 the Australian Army had to be more self-sufficient and adaptable than ever before. It met unprecedented challenges in every military area, from tactics to supply and technology.

More than 730,000 Australians enlisted in the army – some ten per cent of the country's total population – and nearly 400,000 served outside Australia. Up to 40 per cent of those who enlisted experienced life at the front. Some of those who fought were not members of the AIF; these militiamen generally fought well, yet the AIF was the army's elite. It suffered most of the army's 61,000 battle casualties, and was at the sharp end of most of the fighting; it is therefore the focal point of this book.

ORGANIZATION

In September 1939 Australia's regular army, or Permanent Military Forces, comprised just 2,800 officers and men. Their pre-war task was to train, administer and staff the militia, which during the war came to be called the Citizen Military Forces (CMF). In the year preceding the outbreak of war the militia had increased in size from 35,000 to 80,000 volunteers – an impressive achievement in a country with a population of just 7 million people.

Militiamen were allotted according to the 'Divisional Organization' created in 1921. On paper, there were five infantry divisions and two cavalry divisions, though government neglect and hostility towards the services ensured that by 1939 these organizations were cadres only.

The unit numbers and traditions of the First AIF battalions had been transferred to the militia in 1921. At that time, for example, the 14th

Militiamen practise anti-aircraft defence at Seymour camp, Victoria, in November 1939. Their leather leggings and Lewis gun typify the obsolete weapons and equipment distributed to the militia early in the war; both were used by 39th Bn in action against the Japanese on the Kokoda Track in Papua in July–August 1942. (Australian War Memorial 000165)

Infantry Regiment of the militia had become the 14th Battalion, the title of a famous First AIF unit, and had assumed the latter's battle honours and colour patch (see below, under 'Plate Commentaries'). The new units were raised in the same individual states of Australia as their First AIF equivalents: for example, the 14th Bn was based in Victoria. In 1927 militia battalions were given territorial titles, so the 14th Bn was also known as the Prahran Regiment.

The 'two armies'

On 15 September 1939 Prime Minister Robert Menzies announced that the militia would be called up in batches of 40,000 for month-long training periods. At the same time he announced that a 20,000-man special force, the Second Australian Imperial Force, would be created to serve at home or abroad. Like the militia, this would be a volunteer force; but whereas the Defence Act stipulated that the militia and PMF could serve only in Australia and its territories (including Papua and the Mandated Territory of New Guinea), the new AIF could serve both at home and abroad.

The government anticipated that the militia would lose men to the new AIF, and in October 1939 reintroduced universal service. Unmarried men turning 21 in the year ending 30 June 1940 had to undertake three months' military training, partly with a militia unit, and then pass into reserve status. The nature of this call-up and the creation of the Second AIF ensured that the militia remained understrength and understaffed. Moreover, the side-by-side existence of the part-volunteer, part-conscript CMF and the all-volunteer AIF would be a central factor in the wartime story of the Australian Army (or Australian Military

Forces – AMF). The 'two armies' policy created structural problems, headaches in the provision of equipment and, not least, an unnecessary and sometimes bitter rift between members of the two forces.

That rift owed much to the earliest days of the Second AIF, when far fewer militiamen than anticipated volunteered for the new Imperial Force. The expected proportion was a half, but in fact only a quarter of the new AIF came from the militia. Reasons for this included higher militia pay rates; pressure from senior militia officers, who themselves faced a reduction in rank if they transferred; and a belief that militia units were as likely to go overseas as AIF units. Nevertheless, many of the best militia and regular officers soon went overseas with the AIF, which thereafter received the best equipment at the expense of the militia; so the latter entered a period of lassitude, that would last until the start of the Pacific War.

Second AIF formations and units

The first formation raised for the Second AIF was the 6th Division, so designated because of the nominal five militia infantry divisions in Australia; for the same reason, the numbering of brigades began at 16. The numbering of battalions was not so logical, however, and would become chaotic. In order to maintain links both with their First AIF forebears and with the militia, AIF units raised in particular areas were given the same numbers as the previous and existing units from those areas, but with the distinguishing prefix '2/'. Thus, one of the battalions raised in Victoria was the 2/14th (pronounced 'Second 14th'), and not to be confused with the pre-war militia's 14th Bn, a.k.a. the Prahran Regiment. Units that did not duplicate the numbers of militia units, such as anti-tank units, were initially not given this prefix, as for example the 1st Anti-Tank Regt RAA; but eventually, all AIF units created during the war assumed the '2/' prefix.

In February 1940 the creation of a second AIF division, the 7th, was announced; and as the situation in Europe worsened in May–June 1940, the Australian government decided to raise 8th and 9th Divisions. The four AIF infantry divisions' main infantry components, and their state affiliations, are listed in Table 1. Over time these regional loyalties were diluted, as reinforcements were allocated with little regard to state of origin.

Initially the 6th Div's brigades each had four infantry battalions, in line with existing Australian practice; but when the division went overseas, from January 1940, it changed to the British system of three battalions per brigade, the three surplus units initially being transferred to the 7th Division. Brigades and battalions were transferred between divisions repeatedly in 1940 and early 1941, often to the annoyance of men switched to later-formed divisions, and with a consequent lack of

Early recruits to the Second AIF listen with various degrees of attention to a lecture at the new Puckapunyal army camp. These 2/5th Bn men are wearing loose-fitting khaki overalls or 'giggle suits', so-called because of their supposed resemblance to the garments issued in lunatic asylums. (Australian War Memorial 000852/17)

Table 1: Main infantry components of Second AIF divisions

Division	Brigade	Battalion	Original recruiting area
6th	16th	2/1st	New South Wales
		2/2nd	NSW
		2/3rd	NSW
	17th	2/5th	Victoria
		2/6th	Victoria
		2/7th	Victoria
	19th	2/4th	NSW
		2/8th	Victoria
		2/11th	Western Australia
7th	18th	2/9th	Queensland
		2/10th	South Australia
		2/12th	Queensland & Tasmania
	21st	2/14th	Victoria
		2/16th	W.Australia
		2/27th	S.Australia
	25th	2/25th	Queensland
		2/31st	All states; formed in UK
		2/33rd	All states; formed in UK
8th	22nd	2/18th	NSW
		2/19th	NSW
		2/20th	NSW
	23rd	2/21st	Victoria
		2/22nd	Victoria
		2/40th	Tasmania
	27th	2/26th	Queensland
		2/29th	Victoria
		2/30th	NSW
9th	20th	2/13th	NSW
		2/15th	Queensland
		2/17th	NSW
	24th	2/28th	W.Australia
		2/32nd	All states; formed in UK
		2/43rd	S.Australia
	26th	2/23rd	Victoria
		2/24th	Victoria
		2/48th	S.Australia

pattern in the numbering of a division's units. This was due partly to some units being sent initially to the Middle East and others to the United Kingdom; but the exigencies of operations also led to divisions being rearranged urgently, according to which units were the most readily available, best trained and best equipped.

I Australian Corps

In March 1940 the government announced that 6th and 7th Divs would form a new I Australian Corps, again based on the British model. Command was given to LtGen Thomas Blamey, a citizen soldier who had been Gen Monash's chief-of-staff in the Australian Corps in 1918, and who had initially been appointed to command 6th Division. I Australian Corps headquarters operated from June 1940, and was active in Libya (after the capture of Benghazi), in Greece (where it briefly commanded a new Anzac Corps), and in Syria, where it took over all operations from 18 June 1941. Corps units raised in 1940 included three Royal Australian Artillery field regiments, 2/1st Survey Regt, three anti-aircraft regiments, three machine gun battalions and three pioneer battalions, as well as numerous support elements such as signals and medical units, workshops and light aid detachments.

From 10 December 1940, Gen Blamey was also GOC AIF and commander of the separate AIF Administrative HQ in the Middle East. Blamey's independence symbolized that of the AIF: just as he was answerable only to the Australian Minister of the Army, so the AIF had its own independent chain of command. Moreover, a charter in which the government set out Blamey's powers contained the seeds of tension between him and the British commanders he would work with in the Middle East: although it stated that the AIF would be under the operational control of the commander-in-chief in whichever theatre it served, it also declared that Blamey should not allow any part of the AIF to be detached without his consent, and that he could maintain direct contact with the Australian government, at all times.

Men of 2/25th Bn training in the Northern Territory, late 1940; their 08 Pattern webbing exemplifies the lack of modern equipment that hamstrung the army until 1943. On their arrival in the Middle East with 7th Div in April 1941, this battalion's only weapons were rifles. The Australian soldier's weapons were standard issue British types, but availability was limited in the first year of campaigning. Throughout the war Australia persisted with the No.1 Mk III* SMLE rifle instead of following the British example and introducing the Rifle No.4 (though in the opinion of some British veterans, they were fortunate in this). The 1907 Pattern 17in sword bayonet also continued in use, and was central to the Australians' fearsome reputation in close combat. (H.F.McCosker)

Militia formations and units, 1942–45

With the outbreak of war in the Pacific, and the destruction of the AIF 8th Div at Singapore, the condition and organization of the militia became a pressing issue for the first time since early 1940. Several middle-ranking and senior AIF officers were sent to militia formations to reinvigorate them; battalions and brigades were swapped throughout the militia, and some were broken up in order to ensure that the most threatened homeland areas were defended by the most combat-ready troops.

Some battalions were amalgamated, e.g. the 14th/32nd Bn, created in October 1942. In two notable cases, the 9th/49th and 55th/53rd, the amalgamations were later re-separated, and the 9th, 49th, and 53rd Bns were sent to Papua (after the 53rd performed disastrously, it was re-amalgamated with the 55th). The 39th Bn was a unique and important case; unrelated to the existing 24th/39th Bn, it was raised from scratch in Victoria in October 1941 in response to fears of a Japanese threat to New Guinea. Arriving in Port Moresby in January 1942, and bolstered in June 1942 by AIF officer reinforcements, the 39th performed superbly in action.

Even when serving in operational areas the militia divisions changed their compositions so often that their headquarters were little more than temporary administrative commands for available units; however, three militia divisions – the 3rd, 5th & 11th – did have some degree of stability during the 1944–45 campaigns. Despite initial shortages of equipment, militia units played important roles in the 1942–43 campaign in Papua, especially on the Kokoda Track and at Milne Bay. However, of the eight militia battalions that gained experience there, three – including the 39th – were disbanded in July 1943, for reasons never fully explained.

In the New Guinea campaigns of 1943–44 militia battalions played supporting but significant roles, particularly as part of 3rd and 5th Divisions. Legislation of February 1943 enabled militia units to serve outside Australian and mandated territory, but the only ones that did so were those of 11th Bde, which garrisoned Merauke in Dutch New Guinea.

Table 2: Campaign participation of CMF (militia) formations and units

3rd Division Wau-Salamaua, Bougainville	*16th Bn (AIF)* New Britain
5th Div Wau-Salamaua, New Britain	*19th Bn (AIF)* New Britain
11th Div NG 1943–44	*22nd Bn (AIF)* NG 1943–44
	24th Bn (AIF) Wau-Salamaua, NG 1943–44, Bougainville
4th Brigade NG 1943–44, New Britain	*25th Bn (AIF)* Milne Bay, Bougainville
6th Bde New Britain	*26th Bn (AIF)* NG 1943–44, Bougainville
7th Bde Milne Bay, Bougainville	*27th Bn (AIF)* Bougainville
8th Bde NG 1943–44, 1944–45	*28th Bn (AIF)* New Britain
11th Bde Merauke, Bougainville	*29th/46th Bn (AIF)* NG 1943–44, 1944–45
13th Bde New Britain	*30th Bn (AIF)* NG 1943–44, 1944–45
14th Bde Buna-Gona-Sanananda	*31st/51st Bn (AIF)* Dutch NG, Bougainville
15th Bde Wau-Salamaua, NG 1943–44, Bougainville	*35th Bn (AIF)* NG 1943–44, 1944–45
23rd Bde Bougainville	*36th Bn (AIF)* Buna-Gona-Sanananda, New Britain
29th Bde Wau-Salamaua, Bougainville	*37th/52nd Bn (AIF)* NG 1943–44, New Britain
30th Bde Buna-Gona-Sanananda	*39th Bn* Kokoda, Buna-Gona-Sanananda
	42nd Bn (AIF) Wau-Salamaua, NG 1943–44, Bougainville
3rd Battalion Kokoda, Gona	*47th Bn (AIF)* Wau-Salamaua, Bougainville
4th Bn (AIF) NG 1943–44	*49th Bn* Buna-Gona-Sanananda
7th Bn (AIF) Bougainville	*53rd Bn* Kokoda
8th Bn (AIF) Bougainville	*55th/53rd Bn (AIF)* Buna-Gona-Sanananda, Bougainville
9th Bn (AIF) Milne Bay, Bougainville	*57th/60th Bn (AIF)* NG 1943–44, Bougainville
11th Bn (AIF) New Britain	*58th/59th Bn (AIF)* Wau-Salamaua, NG 1943–44, Bougainville
14th/32nd Bn (AIF) New Britain	*61st Bn (AIF)* Milne Bay, Bougainville
15th Bn (AIF) Wau-Salamaua, Bougainville	*62nd Bn (AIF)* Merauke

Notes:
(1) The AIF suffix was granted to those CMF units of which 65 per cent of the war establishment or 75 per cent of the actual strength volunteered to transfer to the AIF.
(2) 'NG 1943–44' refers to fighting in mainland New Guinea.

In 1945 the CMF operated in mainland New Guinea and the mandated islands of New Britain and Bougainville. Table 2 lists the campaign participation of all the CMF formations and units that saw action.

The shift of focus of the Australian war effort from the Middle East to the Pacific in 1942 brought changes not only to the CMF but also to the entire Australian Military Forces. The AIF brought back with it in 1942 and 1943 the prestige and experience of half a dozen tough campaigns. It was swamped with volunteers after Japan entered the war, and by September 1943 had more than 265,000 members – well over twice the war establishment of the militia. More than 200,000 militiamen transferred to the AIF in the course of the war, many while remaining in their CMF units. If sufficient members of a CMF unit volunteered for AIF terms of service – 65 per cent of its war establishment or 75 per cent its strength – that unit could become an AIF unit, designated e.g. 24th Bn (AIF). As a result, by mid-1942 the infantry comprised three different categories of battalions: the original militia units; units raised as part of the Second AIF; and militia units that had been given AIF status.

AMF expansion and reorganization, 1942–45
The return of the AIF to Australia coincided with the arrival of the US Army, whose 41st and 32nd Inf Divs arrived in 1942. General Douglas MacArthur commanded them and, from April 1942, all Australian forces in the newly formed South-West Pacific Area (SWPA). General Blamey, now C-in-C Australian Military Forces, was given command of Allied Land Forces in the SWPA, but MacArthur ensured that in practice Blamey commanded Australians only. He also ensured that Australians were greatly underrepresented in the SWPA General Headquarters,

despite the fact that until 1944 MacArthur's field army was mainly Australian, and was therefore governed by doctrine and methods quite different from American practice.

The AMF that Blamey commanded was a huge force by Australian standards: in June 1942 it consisted of one armoured, two motorized and ten infantry divisions, in First and Second Armies and I, II and III Corps. Blamey recognized that maintaining this force would stretch Australian manpower reserves to the limit, and once the danger of Japanese invasion passed it was reduced in size. By August 1945 there were six divisions and one armoured brigade, although the 'tail' that supported these formations had grown, and the AMF was still one of the largest Allied armies in proportion to population. All the Australian fighting in the SWPA was done by the three AIF infantry divisions (6th, 7th & 9th), the three CMF divisions (3rd, 5th & 11th), and other army, corps and unattached units.

New Guinea Force was an important command during the 1942–1944 operations. Created in April 1942, it directed – at least nominally – all operations in that theatre until its responsibilities were assumed by First Australian Army in October 1944. Its successive commanders were: MajGen B.M.Morris (April–July 1942); LtGen S.F.Rowell (July–

LEFT **Troopers of 2/6th Armd Regt bring in dead and wounded tank crewmen at Buna, New Guinea, late 1942; the two men in front are wearing the Australian Armoured Corps two-piece overall (see Plate F2). Developments in Europe prompted the Australian government in January 1941 to create the 1st Armd Div within the Second AIF. Owing to the changing nature of the war it was destined never to see action as a formation, but various armoured units made substantial contributions to the Pacific campaigns dispersed in the infantry support role. (Australian War Memorial 013992)**

BELOW **25th Bn men prepare to attack Pearl Ridge, Bougainville, in December 1944; their unit subsequently swept an entire Japanese battalion off the ridge. The helmets and face-paint are unusual. Corporal Carter (far left) would die in the attack. (Australian War Memorial 077894)**

LEFT **At the Jungle Warfare Training Centre at Canungra, Queensland, trainees prepare to jump 20ft into water in full kit. From December 1942 nearly all reinforcements to fighting units passed through this severe four-week course. (Australian War Memorial 060636)**

RIGHT **LtGen Thomas Blamey, GOC AIF (left), Prime Minister Robert Menzies, and MajGen John Lavarack, GOC 7th Div, at a marchpast by that division in Palestine. Blamey, an outstanding administrator, would become the only field marshal in Australian history, but was unpopular with his troops. He could be ruthless with subordinates, including Lavarack, who demonstrated expertise at Tobruk and in Syria, but by 1943 had been relegated to obscurity. The Lavarack/Blamey rivalry epitomizes the tension between the regular Staff Corps – Lavarack was a former Chief of the General Staff – and citizen-soldiers like Blamey. (Australian War Memorial 005797)**

September 1942) – a regular officer whose dismissal by Gen Blamey was controversial; LtGen Sir Edmund Herring (September 1942–October 1943); LtGen Sir Leslie Morshead (November 1943–May 1944); and LtGen S.G.Savige (May–October 1944).

In most of this campaigning a new divisional organization was employed. The AIF divisions fought in late 1942 and early 1943 using the British organization they had adopted in the Middle East. The militia units used a 1941 Australian organization that included a headquarters company, four rifle companies and a machine-gun company in each battalion. These jungle campaigns suggested that the existing organizations were unsuitable for fighting in the tropics; consequently, while the armoured division and the infantry divisions defending Australia would maintain their orders of battle, five (and ultimately six) divisions were reorganized as 'jungle divisions'. Table 3 allows a comparison of the two types of division. The jungle division had an establishment of 13,118 men – some 4,000 fewer than the standard formation. The impact of this rare Australian innovation fell particularly on administrative, transport and artillery elements.

The number of artillery (and especially AA) units multiplied in the early war years, and by June 1942 some 80,000 of the 406,000 members of the AMF were artillerymen. In the Middle East the three field regiments attached to each division were essential; but in the Pacific the difficulty of transporting guns and maintaining ammunition supply led to a drastic reduction in field artillery. Only one field regiment per division was considered viable, and the other highly trained and well-equipped regiments were either allocated to other commands or, more often, left

Table 3: Organization of Australian divisions

Arm/branch	Standard Division	Jungle Division
Cavalry	cav regt	cav (commando) regt
Artillery	HQ RAA	HQ RAA
	3× fld regts	1× fld regt
	1× lt AA regt	1 LAA bty (airborne)
	1× AT regt	
	1× survey bty	
Engineers	HQ RAE	HQ RAE
	3× fld coys	3× fld coys
	1× fld park coy	1× fld park coy
	camouflage training unit	camo trng unit
Signals	3× coys	3× coys
Infantry	3× bdes	3× bdes
Service Corps	HQ AASC	HQ AASC
	3× coys	2× coys
Medical Corps	3× fld ambulances	3× fld ambs
Ordnance	3× bde ord fld parks	3× bde ord fld pks
	mobile laundry	
Elec & Mech Engineers (AEME)	10× light aid dets	6× LADs
	3× bde workshops	3× bde wkshps
	LAA regt wkshp	
Miscellaneous	provost coy	provost coy
	div postal unit	div postal unit
	div salvage unit	div salvage unit
	fld cash office	fld cash office
	div reception camp	div recep camp
	div concert party	

Infantry battalion headquarters companies

Within infantry bns the standard British arrangement of 4× rifle coys plus an HQ Coy persisted, but within HQ Coys major changes followed alterations in doctrine and conditions. Configurations varied slightly between battalions, but typical designations were as follows:

Platoon No.	1941 designation	1943 designation
1.	Signals	Signals
2.	Anti-aircraft	Medium machine gun
3.	Mortar	Mortar
4.	Carrier	Tank-attack
5.	Pioneer	Pioneer
6.	Transport	Transport (reduced by ⅔)

languishing in Australia. Only in the 1944–45 campaigns were these superb units, including the AT regiments, re-allocated to their divisions.

Aircraft and native porters necessarily replaced trucks as the infantry divisions' main means of transport in the tropics. The natives were conscripted labourers, whose invaluable work as stretcher-bearers, supply carriers and general labourers has entered Australian folklore. In both Papua and New Guinea they were directed by ANGAU (the Australian New Guinea Administrative Unit), which also recruited native soldiers.

The organization of the Australian Army fostered rifts between AIF and militia, despite government attempts to minimize the differences. There was an organizational schism between pre-war staff officers and militia officers. Australia's dependence on the British model, particularly in the existence of separate facilities for officers and the position of batman, ran counter to the egalitarianism on which Australians prided themselves. Nevertheless, from 1942 careers were largely open to talent; and deficiencies in the AMF's organization did not prevent it from recording far more operational successes than reverses.

The Papuan Infantry Battalion, comprising Papuans and volunteer Australian officers and senior NCOs, fought the Japanese from 1942, and 1st and 2nd New Guinea Inf Bns were raised in 1944; together the three units – each comprising 77 Australians and about 550 native soldiers – formed the Pacific Islands Regiment. Two more battalions had begun enlisting by the end of the war, and the growth of this small New Guinea army partially offset reductions in the CMF and AIF.

Here Capt Grahamslaw, of ANGAU, briefs SgtMaj Katue of the Papuan Inf Bn before a patrol near Buna in October 1942. Katue, a pre-war policeman, was an extraordinary patroller; by this date he had received a Military Medal for work which included killing 26 Japanese and capturing one. His uniform and equipment include a field service cap and sleeveless jumper; a painting shows him wearing a shirt on which he stitched rank badges from four Japanese he had killed. See also Plate G1. (Australian War Memorial 127566)

Australian nurses tend casualties of the Kokoda campaign. Members of the Australian Army Nursing Service (AANS) served wherever the rest of the AIF did, and 71 were killed. Women also served in the Australian Army Medical Women's Service (AAMWS) as ward and theatre assistants and medical technicians. In the Australian Women's Army Service (AWAS) women performed numerous auxiliary roles such as drivers, clerks and signallers. (Australian War Memorial 013503)

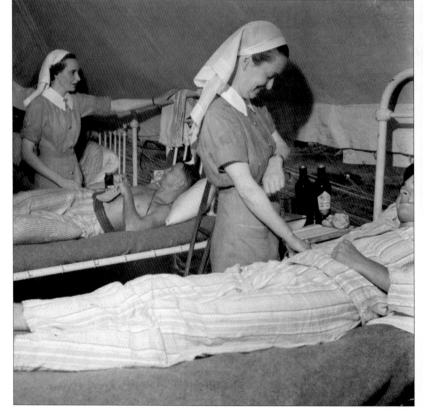

CAMPAIGNS

Bardia to Benghazi (December 1940–February 1941)

The Second AIF's initiation into battle occurred at Bardia, Libya, on 3 January 1941. An Italian thrust into Egypt had been repulsed; Gen O'Connor's Western Desert Force had taken the offensive, and in December 1940 the 6th Australian Div replaced 4th Indian Div as its main infantry component. In the subsequent assault on the Italian fortress of Bardia, Australian infantry and British armour achieved a great combined-arms success; within three days they had captured Bardia, together with more than 40,000 Italians and masses of equipment. More than 90 per cent of the 500 casualties sustained by the Commonwealth forces were Australian, but the 6th Div commander, Gen Mackay, freely acknowledged that the Matilda tanks of LtCol Jerram's 7 RTR had been crucial. Mutual admiration among British and Australian fighting men was a theme of this campaign (although some senior British officers were annoyed by what they considered slack Australian discipline during the post-victory celebrations).

The capture of a second Italian fortress, Tobruk, on 21/22 January was another triumph of British and Australian co-operation. Australians planned the battle and again suffered the bulk of the casualties. The

A Matilda tank of 2/4th Armd Regt on the Buin Road, Bougainville, in 1945. Matildas were long obsolete by European standards, and all tanks were restricted by jungle terrain; nevertheless, with their heavy armour and useful 2-pdr gun (or a flame-thrower, in the Mk IV 'Frog' modification), various versions made telling contributions to 'bunker-busting' in Borneo, New Guinea and Bougainville. (Australian War Memorial 092463)

January 1941: troopers of 6th Div Cav Regt rest in front of their overloaded and camouflaged Universal carrier at Derna, which the Italians had just vacated after a stiff fight. A cavalry colour patch (see Plate H17) is just visible on the right shoulder of the centre man – who also shows what the desert did to the appearance of Australian boots. Although British troops admired the Australians' fighting qualities, some senior officers criticized them for looting and general indiscipline; on asking the British commander in Cyrenaica, Gen Maitland Wilson, what he thought of the Australians, Prime Minister Menzies was taken aback to hear: 'They're troublesome, you know.' Menzies responded: 'I understand the Italians have found them very troublesome.' (Australian War Memorial 044257)

attackers took some 25,000 prisoners and captured about 200 vehicles, which proved useful in the subsequent chase across Cyrenaica. On 7 February, Benghazi surrendered to the Australians, whose forces had advanced nearly 600km (375 miles) in little more than a month. Australian forces went beyond Benghazi, but impending operations elsewhere and the need to rest and refit halted the advance. The 6th Div was withdrawn for service in Greece, and replaced by the ill-equipped and only partially trained 9th Division.

When Gen Rommel's newly arrived German forces thrust into Cyrenaica in March 1941 they soon drove the few British forces and the 9th Div from their defences and back towards the Egyptian border. Most of the Australians and some British units reached the relative safety of Tobruk, but by 11 April that port was surrounded.

The Siege of Tobruk (April–December 1941)

For most of the eight-month siege the defenders were predominantly Australian: 9th Div (less most of its artillery and its cavalry regiment), as well as 18th Bde from 7th Div and various corps troops. In general the Australians manned the perimeter, and British troops most of the supporting weapons, including the vital artillery. Command was in the hands of Australians until October. Major-General Lavarack, GOC Cyrenaica Command, organized the defence against the first Axis attack on 13 April, and thereafter MajGen Leslie Morshead performed prodigies as fortress commander. Assuring his men that Tobruk would be no Dunkirk, he instigated aggressive patrolling and raiding that constantly challenged the enemy.

When the Germans achieved a breakthrough at Tobruk's highest point, Ras el Medauuar, on 1 May, Morshead threw sufficient forces into the breach to enable his men to dig a new makeshift line that held throughout the siege. The Salient thus created pitted Australians and Axis troops against one another at such close range that movement above ground in daylight usually meant instant death.

Australians demonstrated characteristic ingenuity during the siege of Tobruk, employing all kinds of captured Italian equipment, including artillery. Here gunners of 2/12th Field Regt RAA – one wearing an Italian pith helmet – are using an Italian 75mm gun. All the Australian and British defenders of the besieged port revelled in the nickname 'Rats of Tobruk', derived from the sneering claim of the German propagandist 'Lord Haw Haw' that they were trapped like rats. (Australian War Memorial P01260.008)

Syria, October 1941: senior Australian officers flank Gen Auchinleck, the British C-in-C Middle East. Though all wear peaked (visored) SD caps in khaki drab wool and KD cotton clothing, the photo indicates the diversity of uniforms worn by Australian officers in this theatre. At far left is Brig Stevens, who later commanded 6th Div; at far right, Brig Berryman, later a corps commander and Gen Blamey's chief-of-staff. Behind them is Hill 1284, site of a heroic but forlorn Australian charge against a Vichy French position in June that year. (Australian War Memorial 020824)

Rommel used some of his best troops to man this area; and during the 'May Show' in which the Salient was created, the Afrika Korps commander described some Australian prisoners he saw as 'immensely big and powerful men, who without question represented an elite formation of the British Empire'. The defence of the fortress was identified internationally with the Australians, but the latter acknowledged the skill of the British field artillery, anti-aircraft and machine-gun units, recognizing that the British 25-pounder guns provided essential defence against German tanks.

The defenders endured great heat, eternal dust and flies, lack of water and monotonous rations. One of Morshead's brigadiers later criticized him for being a bit 'last war' in his unwillingness ever to yield ground. Colloquially known as 'Ming the Merciless', the disciplinarian Morshead did send his men into some hopeless attacks; moreover, the gruelling round of patrols was mentally draining. From July, Gen Blamey urged a relief of the Australians, whom he considered physically run down; his government supported this request, and there followed a good deal of argument with their British counterparts. The Australian leaders prevailed, and their men were withdrawn by sea between August and October (though one battalion, the 2/13th, missed out as its convoy had to turn back).

Greece and Crete (April–May 1941)

While 9th Div held Tobruk, 6th Div joined the British, New Zealand and Greek forces defending Greece, where the Australian and New Zealand divisions were briefly reunited in an Anzac Corps. When the Germans attacked, only part of 6th Div had arrived in the north. The Germans' overwhelming superiority in numbers and weapons ensured a rapid Allied withdrawal in harsh weather and terrain, and within nine days the British commanders had decided that an evacuation was unavoidable. For several days Australian troops played a prominent part in a holding action on the Thermopylae Line in southern Greece, allowing ships to be assembled to evacuate thousands to Egypt and Crete on 24–27 April 1941.

Pte Armstrong of 2/3rd Bn, 16th Bde, 6th Div in Alexandria after the evacuation from Greece. Unshaven, wounded, and wearing a mixture of winter and summer uniform, he was on the losing side this time – but he still has his Thompson gun. The 6th Div lost some 6,500 men in Greece and Crete, but its rebuilt brigades would go on to fight effectively in New Guinea. (Australian War Memorial 008175)

On Crete, several thousand Australians fought in their original units or new agglomerations against the German airborne invasion that began on 20 May. Like all the defenders, they were short of arms and equipment; but in the ferocious fighting at Retimo and Heraklion they held their own until German reinforcements came up. During the retreat across the island Australians contributed to the desperately tired but effective rearguard. The Australians lost some 2,000 captured in Greece, and 3,000 in Crete, and these operations cost Australia some 600 killed and 1,000 wounded. It was a campaign that embittered the surviving veterans, who directed their anger at British politicians and generals, Blamey, and the RAF, as well as at the Germans.

Syria and Lebanon (June–July 1941)

On 8 June 1941, at the insistence of the British government, Gen Wavell launched a hastily planned invasion of Vichy-held Lebanon and Syria. Most of the troops were Australians of 7th Div, who spearheaded two of the three columns that attacked from Palestine and Transjordan.

Although assured that the Vichy French would offer little resistance, they soon found themselves attacking thoroughly prepared defences that exploited the mountainous terrain; the columns were not mutually supporting, and made variable progress. After a week of fighting the French defenders counter-attacked, exploiting their superiority in armour; the counter-attack soon foundered against stubborn defence, but it disrupted the Allied timetable by several days.

On 18 June, Gen Lavarack, now commanding I Australian Corps, took over the campaign from the British Gen Wilson. He wisely decided to concentrate the attack on the coastal sector, where Australians fought the decisive battle on 5–9 July at Damour; this involved a frontal attack across the Damour river as well as fighting in rugged country to the east of the town. Australians also did most of the fighting in the central sector, especially around Merdjayoun and Jezzine, and contributed to the advance in the east once the Allied forces took Damascus.

With Beirut threatened the Vichy command sought an armistice, and hostilities ceased on 12 July; the campaign had cost the Australians 1,500 killed and wounded. Australian participants felt (justifiably) that the British and Australian authorities intentionally restricted publicity about their efforts in this tough campaign, which was politically sensitive.

El Alamein (July–November 1942)

When a South African garrison surrendered Tobruk to Rommel in June 1942, the only Australian division still in the Middle East was the 9th, on garrison duty in Syria. Appalled to hear of the sudden loss of the town they had fought so hard to defend in 1941, they were soon disappointed again when Rommel's further advance led to the 9th returning to Egypt rather than following the other Australian divisions home.

By the time 9th Div arrived the Axis advance had been halted; but it won a significant victory on 10 July, when it captured high ground on the coast overlooking a vast area near El Alamein, overran an Italian division and destroyed a crucial German intelligence unit. Thereafter the division participated in savage fighting around the Tel el Eisa and Miteiriya Ridges. These July operations cost the Australians 2,552 battle casualties, but they won important ground for the impending Allied offensive.

Mail distribution to 2/3rd Pioneer Bn on the El Alamein line, August 1942; this unit, one of four pioneer battalions, would receive a bloody introduction to battle that October. With no prospect of regular home leave, Australians in the Middle East always longed for mail. Like the man at second left, several members of the battalion found and wore Afrika Korps field caps after being unwisely ordered to leave their slouch hats in Palestine. (Peter Bannigan)

Malaya, January 1942: two 2/15th Field Regt gunners place a stuffed mascot on a truck – note the 8th Div's emu sign partly visible on the mudguard at far right. In all their campaigns the Australian artillery operated in hot climates, so gun crews often fought shirtless. As non-infantrymen both soldiers have been issued 37 Pattern webbing 'cartridge carriers' in place of basic pouches. Gunner Martin (left) would be one of the nearly 8,000 Australian prisoners of war to die in Japanese captivity. (Australian War Memorial 011303/31)

August 1942: five officers of 2/14th Bn, 21st Bde pose at Uberi at the beginning of the Kokoda Track. Even this early in the Papuan campaign officers were carrying rifles and removing rank badges to confuse enemy snipers; nevertheless, all of these five would become casualties in the succeeding months, and only Lt Mason (second from right) would survive 1942. (Australian War Memorial P00525.006)

When that offensive opened on 23 October the Australians were still on the right of the line, astride the coast road. They played a critical role, especially when, after their capture of Trig 29 (Hill 28 to the Germans), Rommel became convinced that the main Allied thrust would come along that road. In fact, Montgomery planned a breakthrough further south, and by drawing on themselves the full weight of the elite German formations the Australians fighting at Trig 29 and around the 'Blockhouse' made that penetration possible. General Leese, the British corps commander, was not exaggerating when he later described the fighting in the 9th Div sector as 'homeric'; the Australians suffered nearly 2,700 casualties in the battle.

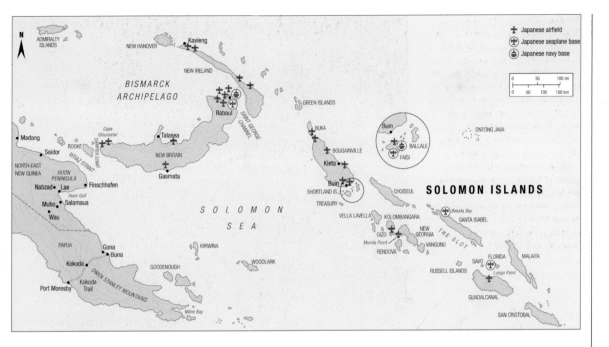

The southern and eastern part of the South-West Pacific Area, with strategic Japanese bases established by mid-1942. This map shows the main areas of Australian operations in New Guinea during 1942–43, and in Bougainville and New Britain, November 1944–August 1945. It does not cover the final push in New Guinea in October 1944–May 1945, up the north coast to Wewak, about 180 miles (290km) north-west of Madang.

The Japanese Onslaught (December 1941–March 1942)

In its first confrontations with Japan the Australian Army suffered a series of disasters, some partly of its own making, but generally against superior numbers and tactics despite brave efforts.

In Malaya, where two brigades of the 8th Div were stationed, the advancing Japanese did not meet the Australians until they reached the state of Johore in the south. The initial contact was at Gemas on 14 January, where Australians inflicted hundreds of Japanese casualties in an ambush. The following day Australian gunners knocked out six Japanese tanks, but heavy pressure eventually forced the Australians back. They enjoyed another success against tanks at Bakri, where a counter-attack also scored a minor victory, but when the Japanese cut the road behind them the Australians had to retreat once more. There was a final successful ambush at Jemaluang, but by 31 January those Australians not already dead or captured had joined the British withdrawal to Singapore Island.

Partly because the Australians had performed well in Malaya, the British Gen Percival placed their depleted battalions – most of which were down to half strength – in the key north-western sector of the island. What followed is a subject of great controversy in Australian military historiography. What is undeniable is that the Japanese landed on 8 February, and overcame the Australians; within a week the 'fortress' had fallen, in one of the British Empire's greatest military disasters. By that time many Australian troops had shown themselves to be appallingly undisciplined; on the other hand, more than 800 Australians fought to the death on Singapore. Prominent among the undisciplined deserters were recent reinforcements – many of whom had never fired a rifle even in training – and base troops. A wartime British report blamed the Australians for the loss of Singapore, but this was a gross over-simplification. Some 15,000 Australians went into captivity at Singapore.

Ad hoc named forces of various sizes were significant in Australian operations, especially in New Guinea, where small groups could play crucial roles. Notable examples included: *1942:* Gull Force (Ambon), Lark Force (Rabaul), Sparrow Force (Timor), Blackforce (Java), Kanga Force (New Guinea), Maroubra Force (Kokoda), Chaforce (Kokoda and Gona) *1943:* Bena, Wampit, Tsili Tsili (New Guinea) *1945:* Hayforce (New Guinea).

Here, four members of Chaforce plod through the mud of the Kokoda Track. This 400-strong unit was formed from the fitter members of 21st Bde once the brigade had been rested in September 1942, but during the campaign each of the men illustrated was evacuated ill, wounded, or both. Chaforce received jungle-green clothing; the second and third men wear cut-down shorts. The abandoned bicycle is Japanese. (Australian War Memorial 013620)

Australian garrisons elsewhere suffered a similar fate. They offered short, sharp fights in New Britain and Ambon in January 1942; on both islands there were massacres of Australian prisoners, as there had been in Malaya and Singapore. On 20 February, the day after the first-ever air raid on Australian soil at Darwin, a Japanese force landed on Dutch Timor, where the defenders were soon overrun. When the Japanese landed in Java in March the defenders included 2,800 Australians, including Middle East veterans. Isolated and greatly outnumbered, they surrendered after suffering 100 casualties; another 716 of them would die in captivity – as would 7,000 of the other Australian troops captured in the initial Japanese onslaught.

The Kokoda Track (July 1942–November 1942)

Japan wanted Australia's territories in New Guinea as forward bases for projecting air power and as a shield for its gains in the Netherlands East Indies. Consequently, Japanese troops landed on the north coast of New Guinea, at Lae and Salamaua in March 1942, and in Papua at Buna and Gona in July. Kanga Force, comprising commandos and local whites of the New Guinea Volunteer Rifles, made guerrilla raids near Salamaua. From February, Japanese aircraft bombed Port Moresby, the harbour on the south coast which was the key Japanese objective on the island. The Coral Sea naval battle in May thwarted an amphibious assault on Port Moresby, but an overland thrust followed the landings at Gona. This was an advance south-westwards along the Kokoda Track (or Trail), running across the rugged Owen Stanley Mountains via the village of Kokoda, site of the only significant airstrip. Australian commanders had considered the track impassable for large-scale military movements; the first 2,000-odd Japanese met resistance only from the hopelessly outnumbered Papuan Inf Bn and the militia 39th Bn, and by 29 July they had occupied Kokoda. By 31 August, 13,500 Japanese troops had arrived in Papua.

At the same time experienced Australian reinforcements from 7th Div were arriving, and on 16 August its 21st Bde set out north-eastwards along the track from Port Moresby. An inadequate supply system, based on locally recruited porters and primitive air-dropping from a handful of aircraft, meant that only two battalions could go forward. The resupplied and reinforced Japanese resumed their attack on 26 August at Isurava, just as 21st Bde arrived; the latter, and the remnants of 39th Bn, hung on at Isurava for several days of close-range fighting that are now celebrated in Australian history. In this action Pte Bruce Kingsbury earned the Victoria Cross when, with a Bren gun, he turned back an attack on his battalion headquarters at the cost of his own life. Despite such determined defence, the 5,000–6,000 Japanese attackers managed to drive back Maroubra Force (the forward Australian units). The third battalion of 21st Bde came up, but it and other elements of the brigade became cut off for a long period; and on 10 September just 307 men faced the Japanese forward of Ioribaiwa Ridge, close to Port Moresby. On 14 September, 25th Bde came forward and relieved the 21st at Ioribaiwa. Japanese attacks forced the 25th to fall back on Imita Ridge, where the Australians consolidated and were reinforced.

General MacArthur, anxious and impatient about the fighting on the Track, urged Blamey to intervene. Like MacArthur, Blamey had no first-hand knowledge of the unique conditions in which the campaign was being fought, and little apparent empathy for the men fighting in primeval jungle on steep, muddy slopes. He would dismiss several commanders, but on the day he arrived in New Guinea (23 September) 25th Bde was already edging forward from Imita Ridge. Now within range of supporting artillery, the Australian infantry found, on 28 September, that the exhausted and starving Japanese had retreated from Ioribaiwa. There was a fierce battle against a Japanese rearguard at Templeton's Crossing, which the newly arrived 16th Bde cleared before overcoming another strong blocking force at Eora Creek.

On 2 November 1942, 25th Bde reoccupied Kokoda, and within a day had the airfield operating again, with invaluable results for resupply and casualty evacuation. The 25th continued to advance, and on 11 November completed a pincer movement with 16th Bde at Oivi-Gorari which killed about 600 Japanese and effectively destroyed their rearguard. When the Australian main body crossed the Kumusi river by newly erected bridges on 16 November, the Kokoda campaign was over. It had been marked by great courage, ferocity and endurance on both sides. Participants would never forget the physical demands of the steep terrain, the constant damp, the ravages of disease and the brutality of the fighting.

A militia patrol from 61st Bn wade through the ever-present mud of Milne Bay in October 1942, soon after the Australian victory there; Pte George (left) had just washed his one and only shirt before volunteering to join the patrol. All three men are vulnerable to mosquitoes, and virtually all Australians at Milne Bay contracted malaria. (Australian War Memorial 013335)

Buna, 31 December 1942: men of 18th Bde, 7th Div advance through a plantation with Australian tank support. While the M3 Stuart (see Plate F) fires on a Japanese pillbox, Cpl Rodgers tries to gain the commander's attention; he eventually made contact by hand signals, shouts and written notes. The private in the foreground wears recently issued 'jungle greens', as well as US web gaiters; note his full haversack and pouches. (Australian War Memorial 014002)

Milne Bay (August–September 1942)

As the struggle at Isurava began, an equally brutal battle was occurring on the far south-eastern tip of Papua at Milne Bay, whose airfields and sheltered harbour were Japanese objectives. About 2,000 Japanese naval troops landed on the northern side of this muddy, malarial bay on the night of 25 August. Confronted by the militia 61st Bn, they made only slow progress, even with tank support, but they did break through a tired, hungry and lightly equipped AIF battalion that was rushed into the line. The Japanese threw everything into an assault on one of the bay's airstrips on 31 August, but artillery and stout fighting by the militia 7th Bde killed some 300 of them and swung the initiative. Then 18th Bde began a skilful advance, which by 6 September had captured the Japanese invasion base. The Milne Bay fighting not only cost the Japanese 600 dead, but also dented their reputation as supermen. News of this first Japanese land defeat of the war heartened Allied soldiers everywhere, including Gen Slim and his men in Burma.

Battle of the Beaches (November 1942–January 1943)

The victories at Milne Bay and on the Kokoda Track doomed Japanese plans for capturing Port Moresby, but they still had about 9,000 men in their Papuan enclaves around the beachheads of Buna, Gona and Sanananda, and were determined to hold this eminently defensible ground. MacArthur was resolved to eliminate these bases before they could be reinforced substantially, and the consequent 'Battle of the Beaches' was a murderous affair.

The Australians advanced on Sanananda and Gona in late November, while the US 32nd Div began attacking Buna. Successive attempts to approach the main Japanese coastal base at Sanananda failed, as first the exhausted 16th Bde, then American units and Australian militia made minimal progress. At Gona, the tired 25th Bde made little headway against strong defences. When the understrength but rested 21st Bde and 39th Bn arrived they took terrible losses in several frontal assaults,

Vickers machine-gunners at Sanananda, January 1943: the dilapidated shirt of the 'No.1' contrasts with the new uniforms seen in the photograph opposite, taken less than a month earlier. The 18th Bde finally forced their way to the coast at Sanananda, under terrible conditions, by the second half of January, effectively ending the Papuan campaign – but in the process its infantry battalions suffered 96 per cent casualties to battle and disease. (Australian War Memorial 030258/02)

but finally cleared the area on 9 December, when 39th Bn's commander, LtCol Honner, sent 21st Bde HQ the famous signal: 'Gona's gone'.

The inexperienced Americans had been unable to crack the Japanese defences at Buna, although they occupied the abandoned village on 14 December, and the decisive fighting around Buna's two airstrips fell to Australian infantry and tanks. At frightful cost, 18th Bde crossed Simemi Creek, fought through to the coast, and took the airstrips between 18 December and 2 January 1943. That day Americans of Urbana Force, having taken Buna Mission, joined the Australians at Giropa Point. The Australians suffered 913 of the 2,870 Allied battle casualties at Buna.

The reinforced 18th Bde attacked Sanananda on 12 January; with American help they took Sanananda Point, and thereby effectively ended the Papuan campaign on 22 January 1943. The Australians suffered more than 1,400 battle casualties at Sanananda, from a total of some 5,700 sustained in Papua since July 1942. The Japanese dead in that period were probably about 10,000 of some 17,000 committed.

Wau-Salamaua (January–September 1943)

The Japanese had lost Papua, but were still aggressive in the Mandated Territory of New Guinea to the north and west, where in January 1943 they sent some 2,500 men to capture the airstrip at Wau. General Blamey was already planning to send to Wau his last available AIF brigade, the 17th, but bad weather and the usual shortage of aircraft slowed their movement. When superior Japanese forces struck the forward Australian troops on 28 January the latter imposed crucial delays, but were eventually killed, forced back or by-passed. The next day Japanese fire fell on the airstrip even as 57 aircraft disgorged Australian troops. On 30 January the Australians repulsed an attack on the airfield, where two 25-pdr guns were landed and soon proved their value. By 1 February the Australians held the initiative, and the Japanese fell back on their base at Mubo.

A patrol briefing for men of 2/24th Bn near Sattelberg, November 1943; note the variety of headgear, and of shades of dye in the uniforms. The man standing second from left seems to be wearing a knotted handkerchief on his head. Men of this veteran unit were entitled to wear the AIF puggaree, but many preferred the less conspicuous hat band or no band at all. Ironically, the only man in this group who is wearing a helmet would die of wounds within a month. (Australian War Memorial 060576)

Even in the dark days of the Kokoda campaign Blamey had been considering offensives to recapture Salamaua, Lae and the Markham Valley. To that end, in April 1943 he built up his forces around Wau, basing them on the militia 3rd Division. This fitted well with MacArthur's determination to reconquer the Huon Peninsula, including Lae and Finschhafen, as preliminaries to further advances. Blamey correctly predicted that the operations between Wau and Salamaua would draw Japanese strength from their base at Lae, which would thus be more vulnerable.

Again, this was mountain warfare, where the determined and aggressive Japanese had to be evicted from successive muddy and jungle-clad ridges by Australian infantry, including the seasoned 17th Bde, two brigades of inexperienced but fast-learning militia, and a significant presence in the form of 2/3rd Independent Company. Particularly hard fighting flowed around Lababia Ridge, Bobdubi Ridge, the Old Vickers Position and Mount Tambu. American forces and Australian artillery were landed at Nassau Bay and Tambu Bay and contributed substantially. The seven months' campaign ended with the capture of Salamaua on 11 September 1943.

The drive on Lae (September 1943)

MacArthur's main assets for the capture of Lae were Australian, although US landing craft and aircraft would also be crucial. General Blamey allocated the task to 9th Div, in the first large-scale Australian seaborne assault since Gallipoli in 1915. Meanwhile, 7th Div would be flown to the Markham Valley, whence it too could advance on Lae. The 9th Div, spearheaded by 20th Bde, landed unopposed east of Lae on 4 September 1943, and began their advance across rain-swollen rivers and against stiffening opposition.

On 5 September, the US 503rd Parachute Inf Regt and a detachment of Australian artillerymen and guns parachuted into Nadzab, where they linked up with an Australian force that had marched overland. Nadzab was quickly transformed into a functioning airfield and, by 7 September, 7th Div infantry were arriving and moving down the Markham Valley towards Lae. They rapidly overcame relatively feeble resistance in the plantations lining the road, and on 16 September entered Lae, just ahead of 9th Division. The latter had suffered some 550 casualties, the 7th about 140, while the Japanese lost at least 1,500 killed. Nevertheless, 6,000 Japanese escaped the pursuing elements of both Australian divisions, to fight on elsewhere.

The Huon Peninsula (September 1943–January 1944)

The unexpectedly rapid capture of Lae led MacArthur and Blamey to rush through an amphibious assault at Finschhafen, which had great potential as a base for operations against New Britain. The 20th Bde, in the vanguard, went ashore under fire on 22 September; although the landing was confused, the troops soon overcame resistance on the beach and pushed inland. A request for a second brigade was unexpectedly refused, as MacArthur's headquarters had greatly underestimated Japanese strength in the area. As 20th Bde marched south towards Finschhafen its flanks became more vulnerable. They were held by skeleton Australian forces, which defended grimly against mounting pressure during a major approach at Jivevaneng, while the main force overcame resolute opposition and supply difficulties to take Finschhafen on 2 October 1943.

Officers and signallers struggle to keep dry at a 29th/46th Bn forward command post near Gusika in November 1943. The corporal (second from left) has an Australian-designed Austen SMG. Despite Gen Blamey's initial preference for it, the Austen was soon overshadowed by the superior Owen, and was rarely used on operations. One soldier is using an American SCR-536 hand-held radio, and three others field telephones. (Australian War Memorial 016297)

'Manpack' flame-throwers were probably first used by the Australians during the Aitape–Wewak campaign of May 1945; this belated but valuable addition to the arsenal was officially adopted the following month, on a scale of 36 per division. Here Pte Willett fires the main Australian type, a slightly modified American M2-2, during the hard fighting for Wewak Point. (Australian War Memorial 091749)

Captured documents revealed Japanese plans for a large-scale counter-attack to recapture the Finschhafen area, and the Americans agreed to transport the Australian 24th Bde there. When the counter-attack came on 17 October a Japanese seaborne assault was quickly smashed, but the ferocious land assault threatened the beachhead; on 18 October, Japanese troops reached the coast, splitting the Australian force. Meanwhile, the Australians at Jivevaneng were surrounded. Yet by 21 October the Australians had regained the initiative; landing 26th Bde and a tank battalion, they went on to the offensive, and forced the Japanese back from the coast. At a cost of 228 casualties, the Australians had inflicted about 1,500 casualties in breaking the counter-attack.

The 9th Div GOC, MajGen Wootten, now decided to use nine Matilda tanks and the relatively fresh 26th Bde to capture Sattelberg mountain, which dominated the area. On 25 November, after nine days of hard fighting against enemy entrenched on the precipitous slopes, the Australians occupied Sattelberg heights, where a much-decorated veteran NCO, Tom Derrick, raised the flag (see page 62).

Elsewhere, a daring inland advance further north by 24th Bde had contributed to this victory. On 19 November, 2/32nd Bn had occupied an isolated hill called Pabu, from which they could interdict the enemy supply line to Sattelberg and Wareo; for seven days the increasingly desperate enemy sought vainly to shift the Australians. By 10 December the leading columns of the two Australian brigades met, having secured major bases at Gusika and Wareo, and the Japanese were retreating; 4th Bde, with tank and artillery support, chased them north along the coast and finally broke them. The fall of Sio on 15 January 1944 signalled an end to four months' campaigning. More than ten Japanese had died for every Australian killed in what was the largest campaign yet fought by the Australian Army, and its successful outcome paved the way for much larger American operations in the region.

The Markham and Ramu Valleys (September 1943–April 1944)

While 9th Div fought near the coast, 7th Div undertook smaller scale but still demanding operations further west. In an extraordinary *coup de main* in September, 2/6th Ind Coy seized the village of Kaiapit, destroyed the unsuspecting vanguard of a Japanese regiment and captured valuable documents. The subsequent advance by 21st and 25th Bdes along the Markham Valley and into the Ramu Valley was barely resisted, and the Australians reached their objective, Dumpu, on 4 October. The 7th Div's battalions now protected the construction of major US airbases in the area.

Signaller Lamb of 2/16th Bn, 21st Bde, 7th Div pauses during the exhausting advance up the Markham Valley in September 1943. In this campaign soldiers regularly carried 80lb loads; Lamb has bettered that, with the addition of his Australian-made wireless – probably a No.108 Set, which weighed 28 pounds. Carrying heavy loads – either one's own, or supplies for forward troops – was one of the great ordeals of the New Guinea campaigns. (Australian War Memorial 057642)

The Japanese held formidable defensive positions in the nearby Finisterre Mountains, through which they were building a road aimed at Dumpu. General Vasey, GOC 7th Div, decided to block this approach, and sent patrols into the Finisterres. They occupied, and resisted a sharp attack on, the valuable Johns' Knoll in October; and in December they captured key positions on the towering Shaggy Ridge. Vasey had decided to take Shaggy Ridge and the significant Kankiryo Saddle beyond it, and in January 1944 his 18th Bde came up from Port Moresby. A combination of effective air and artillery support, subtle use of various approaches, thorough patrolling and breathtaking courage on the almost sheer ridges brought the capture of Shaggy Ridge and Kankiryo Saddle by 26 January 1944. The militia 15th Bde then relieved the 18th and pushed on to Bogadjim on the coast, where they joined forces with the Americans. On 24 April the Australians entered Madang, thus securing the Huon Peninsula.

The Final Campaigns

At the beginning of 1944, Gen MacArthur had three Australian and one American corps at his disposal; by September the figures were two Australian and five American. In order to concentrate his far–flung American divisions for the reconquest of the Philippines, he sent the First Australian Army (3rd, 5th, 6th & 11th Divs) to relieve those forces then in New Britain, Bougainville and the New Guinea mainland. General Blamey decided to use these formations aggressively, but plans for I Australian Corps (7th & 9th Divs) remained uncertain.

Aitape–Wewak (October 1944–August 1945)

The 6th Div took over from US forces defending Aitape and isolated outposts; Australian intentions were initially modest, as it was believed that the division might be called to join I Corps in operations further north. However, Blamey and the 6th Div GOC, Gen Stevens, were keen to give their long-idle veterans a substantial task, and from late November their role escalated from launching harassing raids, to a limited offensive, and ultimately to an all-out advance on the Japanese base at Wewak. The enemy greatly outnumbered the Australians, but the latter were far superior in supplies, equipment, aircraft and naval support. Even so, it was a campaign run on a shoestring, and shortages of ammunition, air and naval support often hampered the Australian offensive.

In parallel advances, one brigade pushed along the coast and another through the Torricelli Mountains inland. Swift-flowing and sometimes flooded rivers were a great obstacle; flooding of the Danmap river drowned 11 men and briefly halted the advance in January 1945, but by February Australian engineers had built more than 40 bridges. There were three weeks' tough fighting for Nambut Hill. The enemy showed his usual determination in counter-attacks, and fought hard but unavailingly to hold Tokuku Pass and airfields at But and Dagua against the coastal advance. The inland advance, plagued by shortage of transport aircraft, parachutes and landing grounds, was greatly eased when in April 1945 it captured Maprik and established a good airfield. On 11 May, the leading elements of 19th Bde took Wewak. About 450 Australians were killed in this campaign, which cost the Japanese some 9,000 dead. Just 269 were captured alive; and the survivors were still fighting when the war came to an end.

Bougainville (November 1944–August 1945)

When the Australians set up their headquarters at Torokina, they estimated enemy strength at 18,000; in fact it was about 40,000, outnumbering the Australian force of 3rd Div and two independent brigades. Here too the Australians decided to be more aggressive than the Americans had been, and soon launched three simultaneous offensives.

Gunners of 4th Field Regt strain to position a Short 25-pdr gun on Bougainville. An Australian invention for use in the SWPA, the 'Short' could be parachuted or air-transported (as the pictured example, 'Snifter', had been in New Guinea). Gunners considered them less accurate and steady than the standard 25-pdr, and the lack of a gunshield left crews susceptible to muzzle-blast. (Australian War Memorial 077279)

Balikpapan, 1 July 1945: Australian sappers clear the way for a Matilda. Two have mine detectors, while a third is about to prod with a bayonet. Engineers made safe nearly 8,000 mines, booby-traps and unexploded bombs at Balikpapan. By 1945, sappers comprised 9 per cent of the Australian Army – nearly twice the figure in 1941. This expansion took place to meet the demands of campaigning in undeveloped areas, and of providing base services that in the Middle East had been handled by the British. (Australian War Memorial 110379)

The central drive never reached the east coast, which would have enabled it to cut the island in two; but it took most of the high ground, from which both sides of Bougainville were visible. Apart from an abortive amphibious landing at Porton, the northern drive was successful, pushing the Japanese there into the Bonis Peninsula. The main offensive, in the south, was carried forward along the narrow, swampy coastal plain. A powerful counter-attack involving 2,400 fresh Japanese and substantial artillery hit the Australians at Slater's Knoll for eight days in March/April, but tanks and artillery helped to smash it. The Australians did not reach their objective, the main Japanese base at Buin; but the original militia units committed fought hard, and by the war's end had cleared the Japanese from much of the island. The campaign cost the Australians 516 killed, compared to 8,500 Japanese.

New Britain (November 1944–August 1945)

The 5th Div took over from the US 40th Div on New Britain in October 1944, and pursued a policy of containment. The main American base was at Cape Gloucester at the western tip of the island; but as the Japanese were mainly confined to a small area far off in the north-eastern corner around Rabaul, the Australians established most of their strength much further east, at Jacquinot Bay on the south coast. The Japanese offered little resistance to a two-pronged Australian advance northwards, based largely on barge movement. By 9 April 1945 the Australians were established across the neck of the Gazelle Peninsula. Vigorous patrolling, from July under 11th Div, was continuing in that area when the war ended.

Borneo (May–August 1945)

MacArthur's response to the question of what to do with I Australian Corps was to send it far to the west, to the vast island of Borneo. In April 1945 orders were issued for 9th Div to capture Tarakan Island off the north-east coast of Dutch Borneo, and the Brunei Bay area in north-west British Borneo, while 7th Div would capture Balikpapan half way down the east coast of Dutch Borneo.

At Tarakan Island on 1 May, 26th Bde made an amphibious landing on the island's south-west coast after a sustained naval and aerial bombardment; they established a beachhead that day, but the high ground overlooking it was not secured until 4 May. The campaign's main objective, the airfield, was captured after heavy fighting the following day, as was Tarakan town. The grim task of destroying the Japanese forces on the island remained, and took its toll on some of Australia's best troops. By the end of the campaign in July about 250 Australians and more than 1,500 Japanese had been killed; the airfield for which the campaign had raged proved to be unusable.

On 10 June the rest of 9th Div, augmented by many other units, landed unopposed at Brunei Bay and on nearby islands. On Labuan Island, 24th Bde soon met stubborn resistance in 'The Pocket', but by 21 June its defenders had been pounded to destruction. Advances on the northern and southern side of the bay brought the capture of Beaufort and Miri respectively, thus completing the task of securing the area. For 114 Australians killed, the Japanese lost at least 1,234.

The landing at Balikpapan, on 1 July 1945, was the last major Allied amphibious operation of the war. Its value seemed dubious to Australians from Gen Blamey down, but the troops (mainly from 7th Div) executed their orders with the same determination and skill as in more significant campaigns. The initial landing, supported by a prolonged bombardment, was unopposed. The high ground overlooking the town, and then the town itself, were soon captured. There was stiff fighting for Manggar airstrip, and the inland advance was delayed by ambushes and hidden explosives; but within three weeks the Japanese had been soundly defeated, despite their well-prepared defences. This phase cost the Japanese 1,783 confirmed dead, and the Australians 229 killed.

AIF INFANTRY DIVISIONS

6th Australian Division
Major divisional units:
6th Div Cavalry Regt; 2/1st, 2/2nd, 2/3rd Field Regts RAA;
2/1st Anti-Tank Regt RAA; 2/1st, 2/2nd, 2/8th Field Coys RAE
16th Inf Bde: 2/1st, 2/2nd, 2/3rd Bns
17th Inf Bde: 2/5th, 2/6th, 2/7th Bns
19th Inf Bde: 2/4th, 2/8th, 2/11th Bns
Division commanders: (* commanded the div on operations)
MajGen Thomas Blamey (Oct 1939–Feb 1940); MajGen Iven Mackay* (Mar 1940–Aug 1941); MajGen Edmund Herring (Aug 1941–Mar 1942); MajGen Allan Boase (Aug–Sept 1942); MajGen George Vasey (Sept–Oct 1942); MajGen A.S.Allen (Nov 1942–Jan 1943); MajGen Jack Stevens* (Mar 1943–July 1945); MajGen Horace Robertson* (July–Aug 1945)

(continued on page 41)

6th DIVISION, LIBYA, 1941
1: Corporal, 2/8th Inf Bn
2: Bombardier, RAA
3: Lt, platoon commander, 2/2nd Inf Bn

7th DIVISION, SYRIA, 1941
1: Light machine gun No.1, infantry
2: Stretcher-bearer
3: LtCol, battalion commander, infantry

B

9th DIVISION, MIDDLE EAST, 1941–42
1: Infantryman, patrol dress, Tobruk
2: Corporal, infantry
3: Machine-gunner

C

8th DIVISION, MALAYA, 1942
1: Sniper, 2/30th Inf Bn
2: Gun detachment commander,
4th AT Regt RAA
3: Motorcycle despatch-rider

D

THE KOKODA TRACK, NEW GUINEA, 1942
1: Rifleman, 39th Bn
2: Rifleman, 21st Bde
3: Corporal, 25th Bde

E

NEW GUINEA, 1942–44
1: Lieutenant, Independent Company, 1943
2: Tank driver, 2/6th Armd Regt; Buna, Dec 1942
3: Forward scout, 7th or 9th Div, 1943

F

THE FINAL CAMPAIGNS, 1944–45
1: Sgt, 1st Papuan Inf Bn
2: Captain, infantry
3: Militia infantryman, Bougainville

G

H

INSIGNIA See text commentary for details

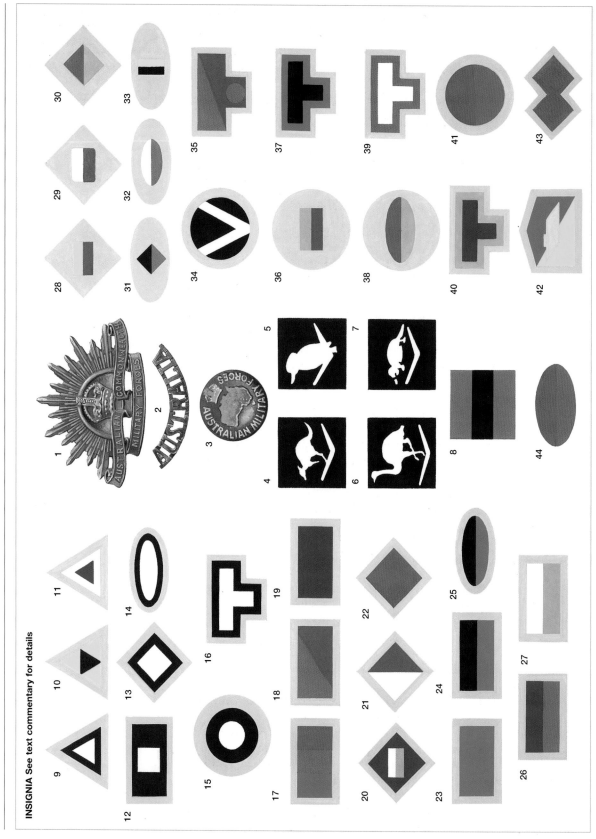

During the evacuation from Greece in April 1941, 6th Div troops shoot back at enemy aircraft from the deck of the *Costa Rica*. She was sunk, but without loss of life. (Australian War Memorial 069346)

The formation of this first division of the Second AIF was announced on 15 September 1939. Initial recruits called themselves 'Thirty-Niners', and took great pride in being the first division raised. Soon after its creation some civilians criticized its members as 'five bob a day killers' and 'economic conscripts', refugees from the Depression and from domestic responsibility. This insult caused resentment, as did the failure of the home-based militia to volunteer for the new division in the expected numbers. Of all the AIF divisions, the 6th contained the highest proportion of 'larrikins', men with a disrespect for authority and a wild streak. Yet it also included a high proportion of Australia's best officers, many of whom rose to higher command elsewhere in the AMF.

The division spent most of 1940 training in the Middle East; by the time of its first action in January 1941 it was highly trained but still lacked equipment of almost every kind. It fought brilliantly at Bardia, suffering just 456 casualties while inflicting nearly ten times as many and capturing mountains of valuable equipment; however, some British senior officers criticized the Australians for lack of discipline in the aftermath of this victory. The 6th was soon at the gates of Tobruk, where its infantry again showed great élan, and its artillery – now at full strength – made a telling contribution. In the advance to Benghazi in February 1941 there was insufficient transport to move the whole division at once, so many infantrymen marched great distances. The successes of the 6th in this campaign gave the other AIF formations confidence, and a desire to emulate them.

The 6th was chosen by Gen Wavell to go to Greece, where it again attracted British criticism, though this time on the more delicate issue of battlefield performance. In truth, the division's efforts were a little uneven – though not as uneven as the odds in this hopeless campaign. More than 800 Australians were killed or wounded in the orderly withdrawal that allowed nearly all the fighting units to be evacuated.

There was no doubting the performance of the division's troops who were diverted to Crete. At Retimo they formed the core of a defence that was successful until events elsewhere forced them to retreat

New Guinea, early 1945: Sgt Daniel (second from left, background) carried this wounded 'native sentry' to safety through enemy fire near Maprik, during the inland advance through the Torricelli Mountains to Wewak. Daniel, who led his platoon of 6th Div for most of the campaign, received a Distinguished Conduct Medal to add to his Military Medal won in 1943. The two men in the foreground have added foliage to their slouch hats. (Australian War Memorial 018695)

or surrender, and the picture was similar at Heraklion, where 2/4th Bn fought well. During the withdrawal 2/7th Bn was the hub of a heroic rearguard, and was consequently left behind by the naval evacuation. The campaigns in Greece and Crete were terribly destructive for the 6th, which lost some 5,000 men captured and nearly 1,600 battle casualties; three entire battalions – 2/1st, 2/7th and 2/11th – were lost on Crete. The division nevertheless went on to make a substantial contribution to the British success in Syria.

Within days of the loss of Singapore in February 1942, the 6th was ordered back to Australia, where invasion was expected; however, it would not fight again as a united formation until 1944. Two of its brigades were diverted to spend four months as garrison troops in Ceylon. After returning to Australia, individual brigades played substantial parts in the New Guinea operations. In the Kokoda campaign 16th Bde took a leading role, and US Gen Eichelberger singled them out for high praise. The 17th Bde halted a strong Japanese advance towards the airstrip at Wau in early 1943, then drove the enemy from major strongholds in the mountains around Salamaua.

From September 1943 until November 1944 the 6th was not involved in any major actions. General Blamey was keen to give his veteran division a task, and sent the entire formation back to New Guinea in October–November 1944. It was charged initially with defending the US gains around Aitape, but the Australians were soon attacking their more numerous opponents, and the goal of the campaign became the capture of Wewak. There were supply difficulties, with air-dropping crucial for the brigade that advanced along the inland Torricelli Mountains. Nevertheless, this inland advance covered more than 70km (44 miles), while the coastal advance stretched 110km (68 miles). In May 1945, 19th Bde, fighting its first campaign since 1941, captured Wewak. The Australians' tactical superiority in this campaign is reflected in the casualty totals: the division lost 442 killed, their opponents 20 times that number. Telling also is the fact that 16,000 Australians were hospitalized with tropical illnesses. Although the political and strategic necessity of the campaign was already doubted while it was in progress, the 6th Div fought as effectively as ever.

This division was notoriously parsimonious in distributing bravery awards; its members received only two Victoria Crosses, both in the Aitape–Wewak campaign.

7th Australian Division

Major divisional units:
7th Div Cavalry Regt; 2/4th, 2/5th, 2/6th Field Regts RAA; 2/2nd AT Regt RAA; 2/4th, 2/5th, 2/6th Field Coys RAE
18th Inf Bde: 2/9th, 2/10th, 2/12th Bns
21st Inf Bde: 2/14th, 2/16th, 2/27th Bns
25th Inf Bde: 2/25th, 2/31st, 2/33rd Bns
Division commanders: (* commanded the div on operations)
MajGen John Lavarack* (Apr 1940–June 1941); MajGen Arthur 'Tubby' Allen* (June 1941–Oct 1942); MajGen George Vasey* (Oct 1942–July 1944); MajGen Edward 'Teddy' Milford* (July 1944–Aug 1945)

Raised in April 1940, its various components were repeatedly reassigned, and it only reached its final form in May 1941. By then one of its brigades, the 18th, was already in action in North Africa; it had captured

Fort Khiam, Syria, 9 June 1941: these 2/33rd Bn men, posing with a captured French Hotchkiss MG, fought heroically during the taking of the fort by 25th Bde; Lt Connor (second from right) received the Soviet Order of the Patriotic War 1st Class for his role here. The respirator case worn on the chest by the corporal (left) was rarely seen after the first Libyan campaign. (Australian War Memorial 008366)

Troopers of 2/7th Cav Regt occupy sandbagged, waterlogged holes at Huggins' Perimeter, Sanananda, in January 1943. Mud-caked clothes became so stiff here that, according to the unit chaplain, 'they cracked as the men walked'. Loud movement was perilous, since the enemy were just 30 metres away. (Australian War Memorial 014211)

Giarabub Oasis from the Italians in March, and was then sent to bolster the defence of Tobruk. Originally raised for the 6th Div and sent to the UK, 18th Bde was initially the best trained and equipped in the division. While it and supporting units contributed substantially to the Tobruk defence, the rest of the division fought its first campaign in Syria, where it provided the majority of British troops for the June 1941 invasion. Despite its inexperience and a faulty plan that spread its forces too thin, the 7th performed well against unexpectedly determined Vichy French opposition, well positioned in rugged terrain around Merdjayoun, Jezzine and Damour. The dearth of publicity given to their achievements was the beginning of the legend of 'The Silent 7th' – a formation ignored by public and government alike. Nevertheless, the experience of mountain fighting would prove useful in their next campaign.

Only in September 1941, after 18th Bde arrived in Syria from Tobruk, was the division united for the first time. When in January 1942 the British requested that Australian forces be sent to the Netherlands East Indies, the Australian government selected the 7th, but many of the division's officers were first sent to Australia to strengthen home defence. As the 7th sailed in February 1942 its men were oblivious to the controversy surrounding their destination. When it became obvious that Java was likely to be isolated, Gen Wavell and Prime Minister Churchill wanted the 7th diverted to help resist the Japanese invasion of Burma. The Australian government and Gen Sturdee, Australian CGS, wanted the division returned to Australia, and luckily got their way. Apart from one divisional engineer unit, which was landed in Java, the 7th reached home in March.

On its arrival the division (with 6th Div's 19th Bde) was by far the best trained and most experienced formation in Australia, but Gens MacArthur and Blamey were slow to recognize the need to send these experienced troops to threatened Papua. Only in August, after inexperienced troops had been driven back by the rapid Japanese advance, were 18th Bde sent to Milne Bay and 21st Bde to Port Moresby. When the Japanese landed at Milne Bay, 18th Bde units drove them back in ferocious fighting. General MacArthur's criticism of the slow progress of the Australian attack was only one of several deeply unfair assessments of Australian efforts that he made in these early campaigns; his criticism of the 7th's performance on the Kokoda Track merely reflected his extraordinary ignorance of the ground and the opposition. The fighting retreat by 21st Bde to Ioribaiwa Ridge ensured that the Japanese did not reach Port Moresby. General

Blamey, fearful for his own position, sacked the 21st Bde commander, Brig Potts, whose performance is now considered to have been excellent. In an infamous address to 21st Bde at Koitaki near Port Moresby, Blamey also implied that the Australians had 'run like rabbits'; he later retracted this slander.

After the Japanese offensive expired, the fresh 25th Bde led the advance back over the Owen Stanley range. It and the other units allocated to the division performed remarkably well, but again attracted MacArthur's criticism for supposed lethargy; Blamey reacted by sacking the divisional commander, Gen Allen. Fortunately the new GOC was Gen Vasey, possibly Australia's best divisional commander of the war, who led the Kokoda campaign to a successful conclusion.

The subsequent operations, against the Papuan beachheads of Gona, Buna and Sanananda, were the division's bloodiest. At Gona a series of frontal assaults on prepared Japanese positions reflected well on the courage of 21st Bde's soldiers, but poorly on senior commanders; Blamey's criticism of the brigade's earlier performance may also have created a 'Koitaki factor', inspiring younger officers to take needless risks to prove their C-in-C wrong.

December 1943: with 3in mortar ammunition on his shoulder, a private of 2/16th Bn, 21st Bde prepares to support the attack on Shaggy Ridge. He has basic pouches and a slung cotton bandolier of extra .303in ammunition, even though he carries the revolver normally issued to mortarmen and machine-gunners of the battalion headquarters companies. This visible sidearm made them targets for Japanese snipers on the watch for officers. (Australian War Memorial 062323)

At Buna, the early failure of the US 32nd Div embarrassed MacArthur, especially when 18th Bde – which he had criticized at Milne Bay – performed one of the great Australian feats of arms by capturing most of the crucial ground. At Sanananda, where the Japanese made their last stand, the brigade won further laurels by forcing their way through to the coast under appalling conditions. Artillery and armoured support were valuable but minimal on this remote battlefront, where the division's infantry suffered terrible casualties: the 18th Bde battalions lost 96 per cent of their original strength of 1,961 through battle or disease. The other two brigades also suffered devastating losses, but a core membership of all brigades returned to fight the next campaign, in September 1943.

MacArthur's plans for that campaign were based on a more enlightened assessment of the Australians as 'magnificent fighting troops, unsurpassed in the world'. The 7th was tasked to support 9th Div's advance on Lae, and to capture the Markham Valley to provide airstrips to support operations further north. At Gen Vasey's suggestion, the entire division was transported by air from Port Moresby to an airstrip prepared just hours before at Nadzab (it was quite fortuitous that the 7th had recently practised just such an operation); one troop of 2/4th Field Regt RAA parachuted in to seize Nadzab with the American 503rd PIR. In a lightning advance inland the division reached Lae first, on 16 September 1943.

Resistance continued to be sporadic as the 7th advanced into the Ramu Valley; but when it entered the Finisterres in October the 1,700m (5,500ft) Shaggy Ridge loomed ahead, heralding three months of mountain fighting. Through intensive patrolling, ingenious and dogged attacks, and not a little dogged defending, 21st and then 18th Bdes captured the high ground and opened the way to the Japanese bases on the coast at Bogadjim and Madang. Though run on a shoestring, this campaign was superbly organized.

A long period of boredom followed the 7th's withdrawal from New Guinea in 1944. Partial compensation was belated governmental recognition of the division's achievements, especially a divisional parade – unprecedented in Australian history – in Brisbane on 8 August 1944. The tedious wait for action ended in May–June 1945, when the division embarked for overseas service for the fourth time in five years.

On 1 July the division landed at Balikpapan in Borneo. Its advance faced stiff opposition; but with air, artillery, naval gunfire and armoured support on a scale that could only have been dreamt of in previous operations, its senior officers could afford to be cautious with their men's lives. A spectacular action occurred at Manggar airstrip, one of the key objectives, where concealed Japanese heavy guns suddenly opened fire on the advancing troops. Several tanks brought up to assist the Australians were quickly destroyed, but a combination of artillery fire over open sights and courageous assaults by infantry and engineers overcame the defenders. By this stage many of the division's troops were young replacements fighting their first campaign, but the 7th outfought its resolute opponents; seven Japanese died for every Australian attacker killed.

The name of the 7th Division will forever be linked with the Kokoda campaign, the most celebrated Australian operation of the war.

8th Australian Division

Major divisional units:
2/10th, 2/14th, 2/15th Field Regts RAA; 2/4th AT Regt RAA; 2/10th, 2/11th, 2/12th Field Coys RAE
22nd Inf Bde: 2/18th, 2/19th, 2/20th Bns
23rd Inf Bde: 2/21st, 2/22nd, 2/40th Bns
27th Inf Bde: 2/26th, 2/29th, 2/30th Bns
Division commanders: (* commanded the div on operations)
MajGen Vernon Sturdee (Aug 1940); MajGen H.Gordon Bennett* (Sept 1940–Feb 1942)

Formed in July 1940 and finalized in early 1941, the division was soon given to MajGen H.Gordon Bennett, who had been a successful battalion and brigade commander in World War I, but proved to be a poor choice. Prickly, conceited and argumentative, he related badly to subordinates and superiors alike. He did not co-operate well with his British counterparts in Malaya, where his headquarters and 22nd Bde group arrived in February 1941, followed by 27th Bde in August. The 8th Division would never fight as a complete formation; 2/22nd Bn was sent in March 1941 to protect Rabaul in New Britain, and the rest of 23rd Bde remained in Australia, ready to send troops to defend islands to the north should Japan attack.

October 1943: this photo, showing two 7th Div forward scouts just metres from enemy positions, was the first taken of Australians on Shaggy Ridge. The Owen SMG has been modified to take two magazines – a feature that would become quite common by 1945. (Phillip Bradley)

When that attack hit Malaya in December 1941 the Australians were in Johore. In accordance with an agreement with the Dutch, in December the 2/21st Bn Group was sent to Ambon, and the 2/40th Bn Group to Timor, both islands in the Dutch East Indies. The remainder of 8th Div was now squarely in the path of the Japanese advance down Malaya. When they first met the enemy in mid-January 1942 the 8th's infantry and gunners achieved some successes at Gemas, Bakri and Jemaluang; however, these were minor and local successes against a background of nerve-tearing retreats that ended on Singapore Island.

General Percival chose to place both of the exhausted and depleted 8th Div brigades on the north-west coast of Singapore, the most likely place for a Japanese attack. This was a tribute to the division's efforts so far, but ensured that it was manning an excessively long front – two battalions over 3 miles for 27th Bde, and no less than 9 miles for 22nd Brigade. The Australians were committed as soon as the Japanese landed on 8 February in the 22nd Bde zone, and after some resistance were pushed back. Bennett prematurely released to his subordinates plans for a future withdrawal; botched a counter-attack to regain the ground lost as a result of this error; and failed to see at first hand 27th Bde's opportunity to exploit problems in the Japanese landing in their sector. By 11 February defeat was imminent.

British writers have emphasized the indiscipline of Australians on Singapore; while its ranks clearly contained some men who ran, the 8th Div suffered heavy casualties on Singapore, including more than 880 dead. Over the straits in Malaya the division had suffered far fewer casualties than it inflicted on the enemy, and it was arguably the best-performing Empire formation. British historian R.A.C.Parker says of the Singapore campaign that the 'best troops among the defenders were in the 8th Australian Division'. In the Malaya and Singapore operations 1,789 Australians were killed – nearly one-quarter of all Empire dead – and more than 1,300 were wounded. The vast majority of these Australian casualties and of the 15,000 captured were members of 8th Division.

Most of the remainder of the division also suffered an awful fate. In New Britain, 2/22nd Bn and the rest of Lark Force were overrun in just a day's fighting, on 23 January. At least 130 were murdered at Tol Plantation after surrendering, and most of the rest died when the *Montevideo Maru*, the Japanese ship in which they were being transported, was sunk in July 1942. The 2/21st Bn met the Japanese landing on Ambon Island on 30 January 1942; after hard fighting at Laha airfield the Australians surrendered on 3 February. In Dutch Timor, 2/40th Bn and the rest of Sparrow Force faced the large Japanese invasion force on 20 February, and by the time the island fell three days later they had suffered 175 casualties. While 1,137 men of Sparrow Force entered captivity, some escaped to join Australian commandos of 2/2nd Independent Coy in Portuguese East Timor, where they carried on a guerrilla war for another year.

It was in captivity that 8th Div suffered its greatest losses: 7,777 men, about one-third of the Australian soldiers captured by the Japanese, died as POWs. The division's commander, Gen Bennett, escaped capture in Singapore and returned to Australia, but his career was ruined.

9th Australian Division
Major divisional units:
9th Div Cavalry Regt; 2/7th, 2/8th, 2/12th Field Regts RAA; 2/3rd AT Regt RAA; 2/4th Light AA Regt RAA; 2/3rd, 2/7th, 2/13th Field Coys RAE; 2/3rd Pioneer Bn; 2/2nd MG Bn
20th Inf Bde: 2/13th, 2/15th, 2/17th Bns
24th Inf Bde: 2/28th, 2/32nd, 2/43rd Bns
26th Inf Bde: 2/23rd, 2/24th, 2/48th Bns
Division commanders: (* commanded the div on operations)
MajGen Leslie Morshead* (Jan 1941–Mar 1943); MajGen George Wootten* (Mar 1943–Aug 1945)

Although this became the most famous and successful Australian division of the war, its origins were inauspicious. The last AIF infantry division formed, it was assembled largely on the criterion of which available units had the least training and equipment. Units originally allocated to the three other divisions eventually transferred into the 9th in early 1941, to the chagrin of most of the men concerned. Moreover, the division's first taste of combat was a demoralizing headlong retreat, the so-called 'Benghazi Handicap' back to Tobruk. The division became the nucleus of the Tobruk garrison during the great siege. It survived the early stages partly because of the Australians' determination and the leadership of the GOC, MajGen Leslie Morshead, but also because of good luck, and highly professional support from British units, especially artillery. The 9th responded to Morshead's insistence on constant aggressive patrolling, which became a hallmark of the division throughout the war. From July 1941 Australian generals and politicians urged that the garrison be relieved; this was achieved in August–September, although 2/13th Bn, which had fought the division's first action on 4 April, stayed behind. It contributed to the final relief of Tobruk in December, taking and holding Ed Duda, a key feature outside the fortress, and thereafter it could brag about being 'First In and Last Out'.

After Tobruk the division went to Syria, where it combined garrison duties with its first large-scale training. When Japan threatened Australia in early 1942 the 9th Div was not sent home with the 6th and 7th, but remained in the Middle East, being sent to Egypt in June–July 1942. General Auchinleck placed the Australians in the northern, coastal sector of his line at El Alamein, where they announced their arrival with a successful raid by 2/43rd Bn on the night of 7/8 July. On 10 July, 26th Bde delivered a staggering blow when it overran the Italian 'Sabratha' Div, took the crucial high ground at Trig 33, and captured on the beach Rommel's key intelligence unit, Company 621.

In the days that followed the Germans sought to recapture lost ground, while the Australians tried to expand their foothold, with their machine-gunners, anti-tank gunners and artillery supporting the infantry against ferocious assaults. By 22 July, when the fighting halted on 26th Bde's front, the Australians still held priceless ground at Trig 33 and Tel el Eisa; they had captured 3,700 prisoners, inflicted 2,300 other casualties and knocked out at least 30 tanks. In the meantime, 24th Bde had been fighting further south on the Makh Khad and Miteiriya ridges. They captured a key point on Makh Khad Ridge; but on Ruin Ridge – part of Miteiriya – 2/28th Bn became cut off from support and communication, and suffered more than 500 casualties, mostly captured. This catastrophe represented just one-fifth of the division's casualties in July. Parts of the 9th – especially its artillery – had not been sent to Tobruk in 1941 and were thus unblooded, but all performed exceptionally well in the July battles.

Australian Army Service Corps soldiers of 9th Div on sentry duty in Tobruk. The AASC's usual role was to store, issue and transport supplies, but in Tobruk some served on the perimeter; note the captured Breda M1930 light machine gun. Both privates are wearing web equipment with cartridge carriers rather than the rifleman's basic pouches; however, after the siege all AASC men who had manned the perimeter were permitted to retain the bayonets they had been issued there, as a badge of front-line experience. (Australian War Memorial 020622)

Apart from a costly diversionary raid, Operation 'Bulimba', the division was not involved in the Alam Halfa battles at the beginning of September; but its position on the coastal flank was of great significance in Gen Montgomery's plans to take the offensive at El Alamein in October. A German assessment on the eve of that battle judged 9th Div as the best attacking troops in Eighth Army, and subsequent events confirmed this. The capture by 9th Div troops of the high ground at Trig 29 drew upon them some of Rommel's best units, as did the subsequent advances north, which threatened to cut off German troops on the coast. Rommel's conviction that the Australians would attempt a major thrust along the coast road led him to divert his armour to that sector, and the 9th's ability to hold them off in the vicinity of 'the Blockhouse' contributed greatly to the British breakthrough in Operation 'Supercharge' further south. The division suffered grievously at El Alamein: although it constituted just 10 per cent of Eighth Army, it took 22 per cent of the casualties.

Montgomery was effusive in his congratulations on the division's 'magnificent' performance, and never forgot their contribution to the victory that established his reputation. (On the eve of D-Day in 1944, Montgomery's chief-of-staff, De Guingand, said to Brig Williams, 'My God, I wish we had 9th Australian Division with us this morning, don't you?') An unforgettable day for the division was 22 December 1942, when at Gaza airport they held their first divisional parade and were addressed by Gen Alexander, the theatre commander, who told them: 'Wherever you may be my thoughts will always go with you, and I shall follow your fortunes with interest and your successes with admiration.'

German radio dubbed the Australian 9th Div '20,000 thieves', and these men certainly look a rough bunch. They are indeed drinking Canadian beer taken from a dump that they passed on the way up to the El Alamein line in July 1942, and one wears a Balmoral bonnet that he swapped with a South African. These are soldiers of Australia's most decorated battalion of the war, the 2/48th; in the forthcoming battles all but the soldier at far right, Pte Bowen, would be wounded, and Bowen himself would be killed in New Guinea. (Bill McEvoy)

Soldiers from 9th Div fraternize with locals on Labuan, Borneo, soon after the landing. The man at left is superbly turned out; the soldier at right is not so dapper, but has employed the old expedient of sewing an extra basic pouch to his haversack. He holds a US carbine, a weapon unfortunately never issued to Australians. The latter's relations with civilians in Borneo were excellent, as suggested by the place given to the 9th Div 'T'-sign in the coat of arms of post-war British Borneo. (Australian War Memorial 018664)

The next field for those successes was New Guinea, in September 1943–January 1944. Although 7th Div took Lae ahead of the 9th, the latter faced more opposition and physical obstacles. Supplies in the Lae–Finschhafen campaigns were poorly organized, but the Japanese were much less formidable than the 9th had been led to expect; only in their counter-attack and subsequent fighting around Sattelberg did the enemy impress the confident Australians. There, and at the Busu River, Scarlet Beach, Jivevaneng, Pabu, and elsewhere the division's four months' operations in New Guinea brought it new laurels. The 9th suffered 1,028 casualties, including 283 dead; they counted 3,099 Japanese dead, and estimated total enemy casualties at 8,000.

It would be more than a year before the division saw further action. About half the men in the battalions committed to Borneo in May 1945 were young reinforcements, but their enthusiasm and the experience of the remaining veterans made for an unbeatable combination on Tarakan and in North Borneo. Three men won Victoria Crosses in these campaigns.

The 9th Div suffered about 10,000 battle casualties in all its campaigns, more than any other Australian division. It also won more decorations than any other; and because 2/3rd Pioneer Bn, 2/4th LAA Regt and 2/2nd MG Bn became part of its order of battle, from 1942 it was also the largest division.

FURTHER READING

Brayley, Martin J., & Richard Ingram, *Khaki Drill and Jungle Green* (Ramsbury, Wilts, UK, 2000)

Glyde, Keith, *Distinguishing Colour Patches of the Australian Military Forces* (Claremont, 1999)

Grey, Jeffrey, *The Australian Army* (Melbourne, 2001)

Landers, Rick, *'Saddle Up': Australian Load Carrying Equipment* (Dural, 1998)

Palazzo, Albert, *The Australian Army* (Melbourne, 2001)

PLATE COMMENTARIES

UNIFORMS, INSIGNIA & EQUIPMENT IN THE MIDDLE EAST

Although German observers could seldom tell British and Australians apart, the Australians in the Middle East did show distinctive features. While most of their clothing and equipment and all of their weapons were of British inspiration, most of them were made in Australia, often with slight variations from the British originals.

As in the Great War, their khaki 'fur felt' hats made Australians stand out; these slouch hats were issued to all ranks, and officers regularly wore them when not on parade or in action. Contrary to some popular depictions, Australians in the Middle East almost never wore slouch hats when under fire; Rommel's ADC did record an incident during the siege of Tobruk when astonished German troops watched an Australian coolly seat himself on the parapet and wave 'his broad-brimmed hat' at them as machine gun bullets flew past, but such foolhardy behaviour was rare. Some Australians wore slouch hats in the initial fighting in Syria, but only because they had been told that the enemy would not fire on them; photographs of men in slouch hats in the front lines are most unusual.

Australians generally wore Australian-made steel helmets, designated Mk III but very similar to the British Mk I* – they differed from the British design primarily in having a straight rather than a beaded edge, as well as in details of the lining and chinstrap. British-made helmets were sometimes issued, usually as replacements. Until 1942 colour finishes were applied in the field, where men used one or more of paint, sand, mud, oil and grease, all with the object of reducing reflection and heat. In Tobruk, Syria and at El Alamein, Australians commonly wore hessian covering on their helmets, and less frequently netting, which was manufactured in Australia from 1942.

While the slouch hat was one emblem of the Australian 'Digger', another was his tan leather ankle boots; when fitted carefully these gave good service, especially after a block toe was introduced. When the 9th Div were ordered to remove any insignia that might identify them as Australians

on their return to Egypt in July 1942, their distinctive brown boots gave them away to the locals.

Rather than the British-pattern battledress (BD) with waist-length blouse, Australians continued to wear woollen service dress (SD). This featured a thigh-length four-pocket tunic based on the Great War design, and trousers with buttoned cloth (later webbing) gaiters to replace the First AIF's breeches and puttees. This combination looked sloppier than battledress; indeed, Australian uniforms tended to look and be ill-fitting throughout the war, and – as in all armies – the combat troops felt that those distributing uniforms had a 'take it or leave it' attitude. Woollen SD was of course often unsuitable for the desert, but it was worn in the first Libyan campaign as well as in Greece and Crete. It was also worn during the first month of the siege of Tobruk, and thereafter the jacket at least was often worn on cold mornings. Pullovers and greatcoats were necessary against the cold of night. Many officers wore lightweight 'safari' (bush) jackets, often privately tailored.

The classic image of an Australian in the desert is probably that of the soldier in helmet, khaki drill (KD) shirt and shorts, short woollen socks and boots; British 37 Pattern webbing equipment was issued in the Middle East. There were many variations on this outfit, including long KD trousers, web anklets, ankle-puttees, woollen hosetops, long socks and pullovers. The shorts were frequently not a good fit; and occasionally Australians were issued 'Bombay Bloomers' – KD trousers with button-and-drawstring hems, which could be worn either fastened up as shorts or turned down to the lower calf.

Australian **insignia** were distinctive. The individual soldier wore oxidized copper 'Australia' shoulder strap titles on his jacket and greatcoat (or sometimes embroidered examples when in the field). His buttons bore a map of Australia, and on his tunic collars and the left underside of his hat brim he wore 'rising sun' badges. Officers up to the rank of lieutenant-colonel – and drivers – wore that badge on the front of the peaked (visored) SD cap; cavalrymen (and in the Pacific, tank men and commandos) wore it on the front left of their berets. Unit colour patches, on grey backing denoting the Second AIF, were worn on both upper sleeves of the tunic and the right hand side of the hat puggaree (see Plate H for further details). The NCOs' badges of rank were worn on the right sleeve only.

A: 6th DIVISION, LIBYA, 1941

A1: Corporal, 2/8th Infantry Battalion

Against the freezing cold of the desert night, the Australian woollen service dress is supplemented with a wool balaclava (probably obtained from the Australian Comforts Fund), a scarf, and a sleeveless leather jerkin – here worn under the

L/Cpl Bridgeman, 2/28th Bn, shows a hole in his helmet made by a German shell splinter at El Alamein. This photo clearly illustrates the Australian helmet and slouch hat, as well as the 'Australia' shoulder title, and the 9th Div's 'T'-patch – in 2/28th Bn, black over red on the usual grey background. Bridgeman was wounded in three campaigns, and Mentioned in Despatches in New Guinea. (Australian War Memorial 029938)

ABOVE LEFT **Well-equipped 2/10th Bn infantrymen are shipped to Tobruk in their baggy khaki wool service dress uniforms, April 1941. (Roger Cundell)**

ABOVE RIGHT **In 'The Salient', the most dangerous area of besieged Tobruk, Pte Rounds raises a Red Cross flag to signal that the enemy can safely leave their trenches to collect a wounded German sniper. Rounds wears a combination of service dress jacket and khaki drill shorts, suitable clothing for a cool Tobruk morning. He would be killed later at El Alamein. (Robyn Smithwick)**

tunic, but often over it. The Australian 'rising sun' badge (see Plate H1) is worn in darkened metal on both collar points, and the badges of rank on the right sleeve only. On both upper sleeves is the white-over-red colour patch of this battalion; see Plate H commentary for an explanation of the system, but note that by this date the theoretical sequence of 'seniority' colours had already broken down to some extent due to the 'triangular' reorganization of brigades. After Bardia, some troops feared that if they wore the helmet chinstrap down they risked a broken neck if caught by artillery blast, and preferred to wear it up or behind their heads. His webbing equipment is British 37 Pattern; the web anklets are Australian, though other men wore cloth gaiters or nothing at all round the ankle; and the boots are the sturdy tan-brown Australian type. His weapon is the .303in SMLE Mk III* rifle, made at Lithgow, Australia. The Australians prided themselves on their skilled use of the 17in sword bayonet.

A2: Bombardier, Royal Australian Artillery

Based on photos and a description in a wartime letter, this soldier is part of an Observation Post party from one of the division's three field regiments. He wears his greatcoat over long KD trousers, without anklets or gaiters, as was common during this campaign. Like many Australians in the course of this hard-marching campaign – and even in Greece and Crete – he wears a captured pair of Italian boots, in two shades of brown leather with a 'half-moon' toecap. On his

upper sleeves and the left side of his helmet he displays a 6th Div artillery colour patch (see Plate H18). He carries the standard issue .38in Webley Mk VI revolver stuffed into a captured Italian holster for the 9mm Glisenti M1910 semi-automatic.

A3: Lieutenant platoon commander, 2/2nd Infantry Battalion

This lieutenant wears an officer's SD tunic with open collar over a shirt and tie, and matching trousers; the superior cloth of privately purchased uniforms was of differing shades of khaki drab. On his collar and shoulder straps he displays the 'rising sun' and his rank 'pips' respectively, in dark bronze finish, and on his sleeves the purple-over-green colour patch of this battalion. He wears Australian issue boots and web anklets; his web equipment for officers has had the positions of the pistol case (holster), ammunition pouch and binocular case re-arranged, as was frequently seen.

The original '39-ers' of the 6th Div were notoriously hard to control when out of the line, but were much more amenable in battle. At the end of the Libyan campaign a captain in 2/1st Inf Bn wrote that 'The men went extraordinarily well, and will do anything you ask of them. Under fire they are continually looking to their superiors.'

B: 7th DIVISION, SYRIA, 1941
B1: Light machine gun No.1, infantry

This soldier wears a hessian-covered helmet, KD shirt and long trousers; few men wore issue anklets with these. In the great heat of the day the men wore shirts and shorts or trousers, but at night in the mountains they sometimes faced bitter cold. He holds his section's Bren Mk I LMG, a weapon beloved among its Australian users, and has the tool-and-spares wallet slung to hang at his side.

B2: Stretcher-bearer

Stretcher-bearers were universally admired in the Australian Army; one of the iconic figures of Australian history, Jack Simpson, had repeatedly rescued wounded men from the Gallipoli battlefield and taken them to the rear on a donkey.

Two or three months into the siege, these soldiers of 2/10th Bn wear an assortment of summer clothing in a so-called 'rest area' of Tobruk. (Roger Cundell)

In World War II it was a hazardous, stressful and physically demanding job, and in Syria these men had to endure great heat and often considerable altitudes. Wearing KD shirt and shorts with socks and ankle-puttees, he carries the standard British Army stretcher folded up, and displays the Red Cross brassard on his right sleeve. Slung from his shoulders are a shell dressing haversack – containing dressings, scissors, morphine and a hypodermic syringe – and a large medical orderly's water bottle with a cup over the neck. Medical bags were sometimes but not always marked with the red cross on a white disc. (In the Pacific the international symbol offered no protection and was seldom used; indeed, some stretcher-bearers went armed in the jungle.)

B3: Lieutenant-colonel battalion commander, infantry

This officer wears the SD cap in khaki drab wool, with the 'rising sun' badge in dark metal. Like many officers he has purchased a locally tailored KD 'safari' jacket; he wears it here with matching shorts, long socks and low brown leather shoes, and without webbing equipment. The only insignia are his rank badges and an 'Australia' title, here embroidered on the shoulder straps in buff, brown and red. His Military Cross and service medal ribbons identify him as a decorated veteran of the First AIF in World War I. Pale khaki SD jackets in heavier cloth, for more formal wear, bore bronze metal insignia.

C: 9th DIVISION, MIDDLE EAST, 1941–42

C1: Infantryman in patrol dress, Tobruk

Even before their first battle, at Bardia, Australian troops demonstrated their skill in night patrols, and at Tobruk they earned a fearsome reputation as patrollers. Whether on reconnaissance or fighting patrols they excelled at stealthy movement. During the siege the lack of water for shaving contributed to the camouflage effect. To help muffle all sound, some men patrolled in their stockinged feet; others wore socks over their boots, and still others canvas and rubber 'sandshoes' (PT shoes), which were issued white and had to be darkened with dirt. The favoured patrol footwear, used in Tobruk and at El Alamein, were these suede, crepe-soled desert or 'chukka' boots, of the type often acquired by British officers – particularly tank men. Rather than risking the clank of a struck helmet this soldier also wears a woollen 'cap, comforter', the tubular item which could be rolled into a warm cap. The one-piece overall was called a 'murder suit' by the Australians. Various accounts refer to 'khaki overalls' issued at Tobruk, and 'one-piece drab coloured boiler type suits' at El Alamein. No photos seem to survive, but doubtless they resembled the illustrated overall, which was issued to many British transport and workshop units. Some men also wore 'giggle suits' (see page 6). To minimize his equipment he carries rifle ammunition in a 50-round disposable cotton bandolier tied round his waist. On his hip he has No.36 grenades in an emptied respirator case (gasmask satchel), used for this purpose by at least one battalion at Tobruk. This veteran has slung his rifle while he examines a potentially useful captured MP40 sub-machine gun.

C2: Corporal, infantry

Cutting out the sleeves of the KD shirt was a common expedient in the terrible mid-summer heat of Tobruk and El Alamein; for the same reason this soldier wears his socks pushed down to his ankles, over boots that are turning almost white from scuffing on sand and rocks. Australians

were generally obsessed with cleanliness, but despite the occasional opportunities to change clothing and bathe in the sea their campaign uniforms were often filthy; men might go without a change for months, sleeping in the same unwashed clothes for weeks on end. The only indication of this man's status as a section commander is his weapon, the .45cal M1928A1 Thompson SMG, at this date still fitted with the 50-round drum magazine. Exactly how its British and Commonwealth users in the Middle East carried spare drums is one of the great mysteries of picture research. Photos do not show the use of the (anyway rare) US-made pouch, and British archives have yielded no reference to the manufacture or purchase of such pouches. The logical expedient would be a respirator case like that used by C1, but photos do not confirm this.

C3: Machine-gunner
There were four AIF MG battalions, and Vickers guns were used in every Australian campaign. This figure is based on Sgt Gus Longhurst of 2/2nd MG Bn, in the action for which he was awarded the Military Medal. At Tel el Eisa near El Alamein on 16 July 1942, as enemy tanks drove around and over the slit trenches from which his platoon were fighting, he leapt from his trench and chased one tank for some 50 yards with a 'sticky bomb' – a No.74 AT grenade.[1] He was unable to disable the tank, but on returning to his Vickers MMG he saw another tank knocked out by an AT gun, and the crew baling out and taking cover behind a rise. In an extraordinary feat of strength, Sgt Longhurst lifted the entire 94lb (42kg) weight of the Vickers and tripod, and with the help of Pte Selmes fired about 150 rounds at them, wounding two and capturing them all.

Some photos show machine gunners in action shirtless during the summer months; we reconstruct Sgt Longhurst after one of these, which shows rough camouflage painting on the helmet, and webbing limited to the .38in revolver case and ammunition pouch worn each side of the belt. His 'dead meat tickets' – the two fibre identity tags – are worn round the neck on a string: an octagonal one in dull green, and a

ABOVE **Australians posing around an abandoned German 15cm artillery piece after the battle of El Alamein; note the variety of clothing and headgear. (David Pearson)**

BELOW **9th Div infantrymen line up prior to the battle of El Alamein. Note the variations in shorts (some very short), socks, puttees and web anklets. Their battalion suffered heavily on 28/29 October 1942, when they rode into battle on tanks. (Australian War Memorial 013653)**

round one in brick red. The spherical tin case of the 'ST' bomb has been discarded just before use, and the safety pin on its tin label has been pulled from the handle. The 'sticky bomb' – a glass sphere filled with nitrogelatin, coated with adhesive and ignited by a 5-second fuse when the safety grip was released – was dangerous and difficult to use. In the same action when Longhurst failed to register a hit, others placed by hand on tanks failed to detonate; yet some Australians in North Africa had great success with this weapon, including Tom 'Diver' Derrick, DCM (see page 62).

THE WAR AGAINST JAPAN

Australian uniform and equipment proved unsatisfactory in the initial campaigns. The pale khaki colour was unsuitable for Far Eastern terrain, shorts offered inadequate protection against disease-spreading mosquitoes, the 37 Pattern webbing became waterlogged and chafed mercilessly – not to mention the 1908 webbing still used by some 8th Div troops. The Australian Army addressed these and other problems with varying degrees of haste and effectiveness.

The militiamen who first met the Japanese on the Kokoda Track, and the veteran 21st Bde of 7th Div, wore khaki drill, and this may have contributed to their heavy losses: 21st Bde lost more than twice as many killed on one day, 30 August 1942, as in its five weeks' campaign in Syria. The men who followed, of 25th Bde, dyed their uniforms soon after disembarkation in Papua, and thus became the first to wear a sort of 'jungle-green'. The *ad hoc* approach to dyeing continued into late 1943, when 9th Div troops dyed their own

KD clothing on arrival in New Guinea. This was one reason that shades of green varied considerably; but even when the manufacture and dyeing of jungle uniforms became more regulated, initial lack of expertise, limited resources, the variety of manufacturers, and a feeling that as long as they were any shade of green they would provide camouflage, all contributed to inconsistency.

In the field some Australians wore American herringbone twill trousers from 1943, but this was far less common than some postwar books have suggested (indeed, none of the Australian veterans interviewed during the preparation of this book had ever seen them).

The 'battle bowler' lost its monopoly as the combat headgear. The lighter, quieter slouch hat became acceptable and more popular for jungle action; as the photos in this book attest, officers struggled to get their men to wear it with any sort of uniformity, and it became shabby with sweat and rain. Like the helmet, it could also get caught in foliage. The beret – initially confined to cavalry (in black), the Armoured Corps (in khaki and later black) and commandos (in khaki) – avoided this problem, and a green cotton version was

P-Day, 1 May 1945, Tarakan: the tactical headquarters of 2/23rd Bn, 26th Bde, 9th Div, gathered around an Australian-made WS 108 Mk III radio. The AIF's egalitarian trend is apparent here; the ranks of the left hand group are, from left to right, captain, private and lieutenant-colonel – the latter is the battalion's CO, distinguishable only by his pistol holster. (Australian War Memorial 090930)

On Bougainville, Pte Henderson of 61st Bn reads his mail after coming in from patrol. He is wearing neck protection (perhaps a handkerchief) under his jungle-green beret, a bandolier and grenades at his waist. His weapon is a rifle grenade launcher with EY discharger cup; opinions varied as to this weapon's value, though it was used sporadically in all the jungle campaigns. (Australian War Memorial 079104)

The British 44 Pattern webbing was not adopted by the Australians, but they did improve the 37 Pattern from 1943 on by making it lighter and introducing a larger basic pouch. Multi-pocket pouches were also designed for SMG magazines, but most men preferred the basic pattern. Broader webbing braces, new water bottle carriers and bayonet frogs, supporting straps and mess tins also appeared, though in very limited numbers; so too did specialized webbing carriers for shovels, wirecutters and machetes.

Men had carried heavy loads of ammunition, grenades, tools and rations into the fighting at Bardia and El Alamein, but their burdens were even heavier in the Pacific. The terrain made it impossible to rely on mechanized transport for resupply, and units were often widely dispersed, so the soldier carried everything he needed on his back. Naturally, what he carried in his pack and/or haversack, and in his bedroll and pouches, was kept to a bare minimum: blankets, towels and even toothbrushes were cut in half to save weight, if kept at all, while other items, including even spare clothing, were soon jettisoned. Only haversacks were taken into action.

The distinctive tan boots remained in service, though a 1945 report concluded that they performed well only 'until operations commenced in SWPA': in that theatre the terrain and climatic conditions drastically reduced their life, the smooth soles gave no traction, and nails tended to rust and fall out, taking heels with them. Some units wore studs from the time of Kokoda, and they were in the scale of clothing by mid-1943. A new tropical studded ankle boot was issued from early 1945, but these were not ideal either. After obtaining his third pair in a month, a chaplain with front-line troops in Bougainville in May 1945 fumed: 'Cross two rivers and what have you? A pair of uppers.'

In truth, no footwear could have eliminated much of the discomfort suffered in the jungle campaigns. Similarly, no clothing could long withstand the rigours of operations in such conditions, despite the fact that from 1943 a supposedly rot-proof shirt with plastic buttons was adopted for jungle wear, and that the Australians were leaders in the field of tropical proofing. The Master-General of the Ordnance admitted in 1944 that shirts and trousers were serviceable for only 14 to 21 days on operations in New Guinea. This report was based on the 1943 operations, during which one infantry lieutenant wrote to his wife: 'Clothes last no time up forward. They just rot to pieces, especially boots.'

The clothing gave grounds for legitimate complaint: in June 1943 an official report on clothing worn in operations in New Guinea criticized its quality, weight and fit. Soldiers in the field reported that buttons were liable to fall off, forcing men to use string or wire to hold up their trousers. Socks were a common source of complaint in New Guinea, where they tended to shrink and creep under the heels. In the last year of the war a

common among militia infantry and some AIF troops in 1945; however, it offered no protection from the sun.

No headgear could keep out the rain that fell heavily and regularly in the tropics, and Australian troops had to use their combination anti-gas capes/groundsheets as ponchos throughout the war, despite attempts to obtain a purpose-made replacement. (The cape was the only anti-gas equipment that proved useful for anything. Soldiers did wear their respirators on their chests when going into action at Bardia, but during the siege of Tobruk their use was limited to some men slinging empty respirator bags on their hips as grenade-carriers.)

The buttoned cloth gaiters and strapped web anklets used in the Middle East proved inadequate against the wet, mud, scratches and leeches of the South-West Pacific, where ankle support was also important in the mountainous terrain. American gaiters (often cut-down) were considered superior, and most frontline troops ignored a half-hearted ban on their wear. As contact with American troops diminished in the latter part of the war, so did the availability of their gaiters. An Australian jungle gaiter was introduced in the last campaigns, although photos from 1945 show some forward troops wearing anklets and others wearing trousers unconfined – probably in the hope that they would dry quicker.

Queensland, October 1943: men of the veteran 2/6th Bn, 17th Bde, 6th Div line up in newly issued service dress before going on leave. The waistband, pockets, sleeves and collar were altered to look smarter, but Australian soldiers had few illusions about this uniform's lack of elegance. Service dress had to serve them for all occasions: ceremonies, leave, battle – even sleep, and burial. Australians coming home on leave in their ill-fitting 'jungle greens' were particularly self-conscious, and resented the impact made on Australian girls by well-paid Americans in smart walking-out uniforms; but the Australian government could not afford a separate 'glamour uniform' for its troops. (Australian War Memorial 058225)

tendency to provide oversize trousers caused especially bitter complaints; perhaps this was in part due to a policy, stated in jungle training courses, that clothes should be loose-fitting to allow air to circulate close to the skin.

The green cotton drill uniforms were designed to be 'all-purpose' outfits, suitable for wear both on leave and on service; they were to be comfortable and of 'an easy style of fitting', in order to minimize the number of sizes to be stocked. However, when men went on leave their ill-fitting uniforms looked ugly – especially when compared to the American walking-out uniforms seen on the streets of Australia's cities. Minor changes were made in an effort to improve the appearance, but it was beyond Australian resources to produce a special uniform for use on leave.

Insignia worn in the jungle campaigns were as inconspicuous as possible due to the threat of Japanese snipers. Although colour patches continued to be a source of pride they were no longer worn in action, except

occasionally on hat puggarees. Rank badges were worn almost exclusively by foolhardy visiting generals, and most officers carried rifles.

When going into the front line from mid-1943 the Australian soldier would typically wear his jungle-green uniform, 'hat fur felt', clasp knife and lanyard, identification discs, webbing, tin of emergency rations in the left pocket and field dressing in the right. Also on the right hand side was his water bottle, while his haversack sat on the left; this contained a tin of emergency rations, a field operation ration and one day's ordinary ration (typically bully beef and biscuits), eating gear (messtin, mug, spoon, possibly knife and fork), anti-mosquito cream or liquid repellent, atebrin anti-malarial tablets, and washing and shaving gear. Except in combat he wore a pack, which would hold a spare pair of boots, two pairs of socks, one or two shirts, underpants, trousers and a mosquito net. He carried a bed-roll of a groundsheet rolled around a blanket over the top of his pack, on to which a helmet might be strapped. The rifleman carried at least 50 rounds of ammunition and one No.36 grenade, plus his share of the platoon's 24 bombs for the 2in mortar, and six grenades for its rifle-grenade discharger. The variations on this basic pattern were numerous.

D: 8th DIVISION, MALAYA, 1942
D1: Sniper, 2/30th Infantry Battalion
This soldier, based on photos, has a hessian-covered helmet, a KD shirt, and has rolled up the long legs of his KD 'Bombay bloomers'. He wears the basic pouches of 37 Pattern web equipment, which for Australians had only just replaced the old 08 Pattern set in Malaya. His unit is identified by the purple-and-gold garter flashes worn on his

Commandos of 2/3rd Independent Coy wear groundsheets as raincoats, but bare their heads as a mark of respect for three of their NCOs, just buried in a dangerous ceremony near Timbered Knoll in 1943. Four of these mourners would be dead within a month. (Australian War Memorial 127986)

socks, which were made and sent to the unit by its Comforts Fund in 1941. He carries a P14 No.3 Mk I* (T) rifle with a telescopic sight – a weapon that remained popular with Australian snipers right up to the end of the Korean War.

D2: Gun detachment commander, 4th Anti-Tank Regiment RAA

The 2-pounder AT gunners of 4th AT Regt won several tactical victories in Malaya. The AP rounds, while too light to penetrate most German tanks of that date, could literally pass straight through Japanese tanks and out the other side; for that reason, at Bakri the gunners switched to HE rounds. This sergeant, who does not wear badges of rank, is handing a report on a recent encounter to a despatch rider. The ungainly appearance of 'Bombay bloomers' when worn at full length is emphasized by the fact that, for the sake of coolness, he has not tightened the drawstring and has rolled his socks right down at the ankle. His webbing has the basic pouches replaced with two-pocket 'cartridge carriers', as standard for many non-infantry troops.

D3: Motorcycle despatch-rider

Australian despatch-riders were a common sight in the Middle East and Malaya; with wireless communications still developing, they were essential to maintain forward communications, especially in a campaign of movement. This 'Don R' astride his Norton is wearing the standard motorcyclist's rimless steel helmet with leather neck-and-

face-piece, but not the leather gauntlets often seen in Australia – few wore both gloves and helmet on campaign. He should perhaps be wearing the white-over-blue Signals brassard on his left arm, but the subject photo does not show this. It does, however, show 'Bombay bloomers' rolled high, with long socks and (perhaps surprisingly) low laced shoes. Non-standard gear was typical in 8th Div, and the photo shows this motorcyclist with the waistbelt and pistol case of the officer's old 'Sam Browne' belt equipment.

E: THE KOKODA TRACK, NEW GUINEA, 1942

E1: Rifleman, 39th Battalion

This volunteer militia unit, inadequately trained and equipped, bore the brunt of the initial Japanese attack through the Owen Stanley Mountains, and earned a place in Australian folklore. This figure, partly based upon a famous photo of men of the battalion at Menari village, is one of the 180 soldiers still on their feet by 6 September. He wears the 'fur felt' hat with a band of the same material; most of the battalion preferred the slouch hat to the steel helmet, anticipating a fashion later taken up by most of the army. He has no shirt, probably because it has disintegrated, and instead has a tattered and shrunken woollen pullover – men soaked by sweat and rainfall valued these, especially at night. His trousers are 'Bombay bloomers' with the legs turned and buttoned up; some chose to wear the turn-ups down, or cut them off, and others wore long KD trousers instead. Below these are Light Horse pattern leather leggings, relics of the Great War peculiar to the militia, and primarily to 39th Battalion. He wears 37 Pattern webbing in fighting order, and the original photo seems to show this as

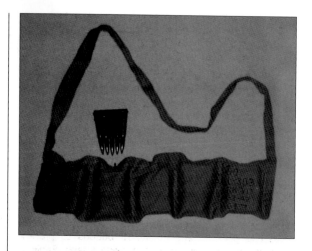

TOP **In every campaign Australian soldiers carried these disposable cotton bandoliers, each holding 50 rounds of .303in small arms ammunition in ten 5-round stripper clips. Ammunition was issued in bandoliers, which were either folded down into the basic pouches of the webbing equipment, or simply slung around the body. At need, the cartridges could be used either for the SMLE rifle or to reload magazines for the section's Bren LMG. (Brad Manera)**

ABOVE **Two 'fighting knives' and cut-down scabbards; dated 1942 and 1943, the knives are converted 1907 Pattern bayonets. The double-edged knife (top) was used by a member of 2/6th Commando Squadron. (Brad Manera)**

darkened in some way. The first company sent up the Track had just one Bren gun, but eight Lewis LMGs; we have made this soldier a Bren 'No.2', so he carries the spare barrel holdall. As in the Middle East, the Bren proved a very popular weapon in the jungle, and inspired some of its users to great feats.

E2: Rifleman, 21st Brigade
Everyone who saw 21st Bde arrive in Papua in August 1942 was impressed by their martial appearance. One war correspondent in Port Moresby was struck by their muscles, their self-confidence and élan, but worried that they were carrying excessive loads, and wearing KD uniforms and webbing in unsuitable colours for the terrain. This soldier is

wearing such equipment, although he has received a pair of long American canvas leggings. Australians wore these in all the New Guinea campaigns; Capt Buckler – who fought on the Track, and led to safety a group cut off behind Japanese lines – reported that his US gaiters gave excellent support, and lasted him two months before breaking at the boot straps. He also reported that shorts were more popular than long trousers, which collected mud and water. Like many soldiers in the campaign this soldier has a hessian helmet cover; but Capt Buckler also wrote that the troops were averse to wearing too much material on their helmets, due to a belief 'that a resistance is offered to bullets which may not be deflected'.

E3: Corporal, 25th Brigade
This soldier retains his helmet, although by the end of 1942 the slouch hat was becoming the front-line headgear of choice for many Australians. The first soldiers to be issued with uniforms coloured jungle-green were those of 25th Bde, most of whom received this hastily re-dyed KD clothing – sometimes still dripping with dye – on arrival at Port Moresby; the results could sometimes appear rather amateurish and uneven. This man wears long trousers and US gaiters; some wore Australian web anklets, others left their trousers to hang loose, rolled them up, or cut them down into shorts. The web equipment was also dyed green – at first as completed items, but later in bulk before making up. Like Plate C2, this section leader has no rank chevrons, but carries a Thompson SMG, here with the later 20-round box magazine (which fitted in the 37 Pattern basic pouches). Although subject to malfunctions due to the extremely wet and dirty conditions, the Thompson was still a valued weapon for the sort of close range encounter

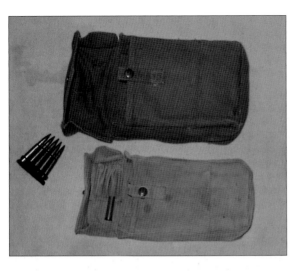

fighting that was typical of these campaigns. Note that he also carries a prized Japanese entrenching shovel slung on a cord. Australians were inadequately supplied with entrenching tools at this stage, and unless they could lay hands on a captured one they often had to dig slit trenches with their bayonets, helmets, empty food tins, or their bare hands.

F: NEW GUINEA, 1942–44

F1: Lieutenant, Independent Company, 1943

This officer wears the commandos' distinctive khaki wool beret with its sewn cloth rim, and the 'rising sun' badge. The shirt of the Australian rot-proofed cotton jungle-green uniform – which began to be issued in 1943 – is worn in combination with mismatched trousers. He is throwing a standard issue No.36 anti-personnel grenade; its heavy fragmentation made it a popular weapon, and some US units were keen to trade for them. Instead of basic pouches he wears a 50-round disposable cotton bandolier for his rifle ammunition, and a captured Japanese water bottle. Three more grenades are clipped to his belt, the safety levers slipped behind the fabric and the ends of the safety pins well splayed; this practice was often condemned as dangerous, but there is photographic evidence for its popularity. Although this man is not carrying much of a burden in action, the independent companies were more likely to take their 08/37 Pattern 'large packs' into the jungle, since they needed to be self-sufficient. (The 6th Div issued its own jungle training manual, including diagrams for making up a patrol pack by rolling the essentials in the groundsheet, then folding it into an M-shape secured with pack straps.)

The Australian temperament is well suited to irregular warfare, and the commando companies prided themselves on being something special. Some individuals chose to express this by means of exotic embellishments like murderous-looking close-combat knives, coloured scarves, and even necklaces of boar's tusks; and after long periods in isolation, such as 12-day patrols, commandos often emerged unshaven – photos even show some individuals with beards and large moustaches. Line infantry of all ranks tended to respond without enthusiasm to the commandos' confident and insouciant bearing.

F2: Tank driver, 2/6th Armoured Regiment; Buna, December 1942

M3 Stuart light tanks of this unit proved to be 'the vital factor' in the Allied victory at Buna, even though they were unsuited to the terrain and suffered heavy losses. Note the khaki wool beret (in this case with a leather rim) and 'rising sun' badge, which tank crews often wore on campaign. This two-piece battledress-style uniform was specially designed for the Australian Armoured Corps. Based on the British 'BD, denim' but superior in materials and finish, it had plenty of accessible pockets, and concealed buttons to prevent snagging on the many projections inside a tank. Sadly, it proved less than ideal in action: most crewmen found it too heavy in the humid heat. Drivers and hull gunners also found that unless the blouse and trousers were perfectly fitted they would not stay buttoned together at the waistband during the contortions that were unavoidable for tank crews, and hot cartridge cases from the co-axial machine gun would inflict painful burns on their backs. These crewmen took to wearing steel helmets inside the tank; and one photo shows what seems to be a khaki bandana worn under a helmet – perhaps made from a torn-up shirt, to form a neckflap? Drivers also suffered from burnt feet: the tanks spent so much time in low gear that heat was conducted along the accelerator and clutch rods, and after up to four hours' driving feet were so cooked as to lead to what an official report called a 'loss of efficiency'. The driver illustrated has acquired a pair of US Army 'rough-out' field shoes with rubber soles, which for some reason overcame this problem. In subsequent campaigns most tank crews preferred to wear standard infantry issue shirt and trousers for the sake of comfort. The distinctive long-strap thigh holster seen here was another item rarely worn after Buna.

F3: Forward scout, 7th or 9th Division, 1943

In New Guinea both sides depended on narrow jungle tracks for movement and supply; the forward scouts who led the way on advances or patrols risked death at any moment, and the job was rotated regularly to ensure that the scout was always alert. This man carries the Australian-designed 9mm Owen sub-machine gun, a sturdy and very well-balanced weapon that proved well suited to the rigours of jungle campaigns (apart from a tendency to fire if the butt was dropped sharply to the ground); it superseded the Thompson during 1943. The close terrain and constant damp distorted the slouch hat, and men contributed to this by shaping them individually in 'stetson', 'pancho villa' and other non-regulation styles. Jungle mildew tended to rot the light fabric puggarees that AIF men (but not militia) were entitled to wear, and also their chinstraps; this man is wearing an improvised (and forbidden) leather hatband. General Mackay, a veteran of both World Wars, acknowledged that for Australians the slouch hat, even though less serviceable and comfortable than the Japanese peaked field cap, was 'enshrouded in sentiment'. This man's shirt and trousers are in shades of dark green – the exact colours varied widely. In an attempt to reduce casualties

One of Australia's most renowned soldiers, Lt Tom Derrick, VC, DCM (right), congratulates his friend Lt Reg Saunders following their graduation from an Officer Cadet Training Unit in 1944; this photo shows clearly the proper appearance of the slouch hat and service dress, with various national, rank and unit insignia including colour patches. Unusually, both Derrick and Saunders returned to their original units (2/48th and 2/7th Bns, respectively) on receiving their commissions. Saunders was the first Aboriginal commissioned in the Australian Army, where he reported encountering less prejudice than in civilian life. By law the Army was not supposed to recruit Aborigines, but a large number enlisted in the AIF early on.

Like Saunders, Tom Derrick was a superb fighter and natural leader who rose from humble origins through merit; the Second AIF gave opportunities for many recruits to exercise leadership. On 25 November 1943, Sgt Derrick – already a hero of North Africa, who earned his VC by clearing ten Japanese posts on the Sattelberg heights in New Guinea – famously raised the Australian flag on that summit. Lieutenant Derrick would be killed at Tarakan in May 1945 – a loss that epitomized the waste of that bitter and unnecessary campaign, which has justifiably been called 'an Australian tragedy'. (Australian War Memorial 083166)

from mosquito-borne malaria, shorts were forbidden in front line areas by late 1943; the ban was observed, but most Australian troops still contracted malaria or other tropical diseases. Most Australians wore US gaiters, but this man is one of the sizeable minority who had web anklets. In time-honoured military fashion he has tied a handkerchief round his neck.

G: THE FINAL CAMPAIGNS, 1944–45
G1: Sergeant, 1st Papuan Infantry Battalion
Led by volunteer Australian officers and NCOs, these troops were superb exponents of jungle warfare, and were particularly adept at reconnaissance; they fought from the Kokoda campaign until the final operations of the war in New Guinea. This figure, showing an appearance typical of this unit and the two New Guinea Inf Bns, is based on photos of Sgt William Matpi, who was awarded the Distinguished Conduct Medal (second only to the Victoria Cross for enlisted ranks) for 'exceptional bravery' on several occasions. The native soldier's dress in the field was usually limited to the kilt-like *lap-lap* or *rami*, which appeared in various shades of khaki; some wore shirt and shorts – especially when on parade, in relatively cold weather, or in areas where mosquito-borne diseases were pandemic. Here 37 Pattern webbing fighting order includes

the considerably enlarged basic pouches, produced from 1944 and standard Australian issue during the last campaigns. These accommodated, among other munitions, the 32-round box magazines for the Owen SMG.

G2: Captain, infantry

With his rifle and heavy load, and lack of rank insignia, this officer could just as well be a private. The tools of his trade range from the most primitive – the machete, to the most sophisticated – the American SCR-536 radio, which greatly facilitated infantry-tank co-operation from late 1943 onwards. He has buckled his water bottle to the hanging flap straps of his haversack to reduce his belt equipment. The informality of officers' appearance reinforced the Australian tradition that commanders had to earn authority over and obedience from their men by their example rather than simply relying upon their rank.

G3: Militia infantryman, patrol dress, Bougainville

By 1945 most of the infantrymen serving on Bougainville had enlisted in the AIF, even though they were members of battalions that had originally been militia; the Australian official historian suggests that by this stage of the war these men had higher morale than the veteran 6th Division. This soldier wears late war jungle dress; note the left thigh pocket of the trousers, seen in some but by no means all photographs. The jungle-green cotton 'beret' – very similar to the tropical-weight British 'cap, general service' issued to some Indian troops in the Far East – was characteristic of the original militia battalions in these last campaigns; foliage camouflage could be (but rarely was) attached through a false band sewn over the hatband proper. On his right side he wears one of the enlarged 1944 basic pouches, and on his left a six-pocket pouch set for Owen magazines – a combination sometimes seen in photographs. On Bougainville clothes were often wet for long periods, to the point where they tended to rot. Leather items such as boots bloomed with green mould overnight, and had to be oiled repeatedly. This soldier wears cut-down US gaiters; as these became scarce, many Australians on Bougainville reverted to web anklets. From 1943 more durable identity tags in white metal alloy became standard issue.

H: INSIGNIA

The so-called 'rising sun' badge of the AIF (1) was worn on the tunic collars of service dress, and also on the turned-up left brim of the felt slouch hat, in oxydized or blackened finish. The shoulder title (2) was worn by the AIF; (3) is the distinctive button worn on service dress. The signs stencilled on the vehicles of the four AIF infantry divisions showed (4) a kangaroo for 6th Div, (5) a kookaburra for 7th, (6) an emu for 8th, and (7) a platypus for 9th Division. (8) is the all-purpose sign for HQ, First Australian Army.

The colour patches illustrated on this page were worn as unit distinctions at the top of both sleeves, and on the right side of the band or puggaree of the slouch hat, during home, Middle Eastern or European service. They were generally of sewn felt; at least 1,200 different designs were used within the AMF during World War II, so this plate is necessarily selective, illustrating only some of the design principles and significant examples. (While studying these, readers may find it helpful to keep a marker in the divisional orders-of-battle in the body text.)

The system was largely derived from principles established in the First AIF of World War I, when the Australian Corps and its units had triangular patches, e.g. (9) I Corps, (10) 2/4 MG Bn, and (11) 2/1 Pioneer Battalion. Within the Corps, the shape of patches used by the first four divisions raised – respectively rectangle, diamond, horizontal ellipse and disc – were retained in World War II; (12–15) show 6th Div HQ, 7th Div HQ, 8th Div HQ and 9th Div HQ respectively, and (16) the new T-shape introduced for 9th Div from December 1942. Within each division the colour patch of each unit was supposed to be of divisional shape: e.g. (17–19) are divisional units of 6th Div – Cavalry, Artillery and Engineers respectively; and (20–22) are 7th Div Signals, Army Service Corps and Medical.

Among infantry units the seniority-colour system of the brigades and battalions was again modelled on the First AIF. The three brigades of the first division raised bore green, red and light blue respectively; thus (23) is the patch of HQ 16th Bde, the senior brigade in 6th Div – the system did not really apply for subsequent divisions. Within units, the bottom half of the patch was supposed to show brigade and state colour, and the top half a battalion seniority colour, respectively black, purple, brown and – as originally raised – white. Thus (24) is that of 2/1st Bn, the first in 16th Bde, and (25) is 2/18th Bn, the first in 22nd Bde; (26) is 2/6th Bn, the second in 17th Bde; and (27) is 2/12th Bn, originally the fourth in 18th Brigade.

The 'triangular' reorganization of the Army along British lines in February 1940 confused the issue, sending 'white-topped' colour patches all over the place. Further confusion followed the many cross-postings during the reorganization of divisions in 1941. Only the 6th and 8th Divs really conformed to the theoretical model of patches, and even those show some variations. Within 7th Div, (28) is the patch of 2/14th Bn, (29) is 2/16th Bn, and (30) is 2/27th Battalion. Among 8th Div units, (31) is 2/21st Bn, (32) is 2/40th Bn, and (33) is 2/29th Battalion.

It was largely because of the confusion caused by expedient transfers that Gen Morshead introduced in December 1942 the T-shaped patch to replace the jumble of designs then in use in his 9th Division. (34) is that of the 9th Div Provost Coy, and (35) that of 2/12th Field Regt RAA. The 2/13th Bn (36 & 37) went through six different colour patches, including these two, which saw it through all its campaigns; (38 & 39) were both worn by 2/43rd Bn, and (40) by 2/24th Battalion.

Three battalions raised from Australian troops in England designed and wore their own circular patches; (41) is that of 2/33rd Battalion. Unit types with no First AIF equivalents, such as armoured regiments and independent companies, had original designs; (42) is that of 2/9th Armd Regt, and (43) the patch of 2/7th Independent Company.

All AIF units sewed their colour patches to a shaped background of 'battleship grey', to distinguish them from the militia; one of the latter's patches, that of the famous 39th Bn, is shown as (44). However, from October 1942 individuals who enlisted in the AIF while remaining in their CMF units were also entitled to a grey background, to which their unit patch would be fixed.

INDEX